Appalachian Grouse Dog

A Boomer's Memoir

Dennis LaBare
Bill Horn
Helen Stacy LaBare

Illustrations by Gordon Allen

Foreword by Steve Smith

CATAMOUNT
PRESS
an imprint of Sunbury Press, Inc.
Mechanicsburg, PA USA

CATAMOUNT
PRESS

an imprint of Sunbury Press, Inc.
Mechanicsburg, PA USA

For information about special discounts for bulk purchases, please contact Sunbury Press Orders Dept. at (855) 338-8359 or orders@sunburypress.com.

To request one of our authors for speaking engagements or book signings, please contact Sunbury Press Publicity Dept. at publicity@sunburypress.com.

FIRST CATAMOUNT PRESS EDITION: April 2021

Set in Adobe Garamond | Interior design by Crystal Devine | Cover by Lawrence Knorr | Edited by Lawrence Knorr | Photography by the authors, unless otherwise noted | Illustrations by Gordon Allen, gordonallenart.com.

Publisher's Cataloging-in-Publication Data
Names: LaBare, Dennis, author | Horn, Bill, author | LaBare, Helen Stacy, author.
Title: Appalachian grouse dog : a boomer's memoir / Dennis LaBare Bill Horn Helen Stacy LaBare.
Description: First hard cover edition. | Mechanicsburg, PA : Catamount Press, 2021.
Summary: A Boomer sportsman reminisces about his youth and his beloved hunting dogs.
Identifiers: ISBN : 978-1-62006-484-9 (Hard cover).
Subjects: BIOGRAPHY & AUTOBIOGRAPHY / Sports | SPORTS & RECREATION / Hunting | PETS / Dogs / Breeds.

Product of the United States of America
0 1 1 2 3 5 8 13 21 34 55

Continue the Enlightenment!

THIS BOOK IS DEDICATED TO everyone who has ever stroked a check, picked up a shovel, written a letter, or pulled the lever in support of North American fish and wildlife and the habitats upon which they depend that make possible our sporting pursuits.

CONTENTS

FOREWORD

IN MY YEARS as a sporting dog magazine editor, those who populate the world of these wonderful creatures get into that world, the vast majority of them anyway, because they were born to it, or nearly so. That is, they were part of a family where wingshooting and hunting over or behind dogs was a way of life. They learned to shoot and hunt early, got their first pup when they were but pups themselves, and their knowledge grew with time and age.

Then there are the others, those who discovered the world of fields and marshes and covers after a lot of life's other lessons had been learned in terms of careers, marriages, family life. One of that sort is the subject and one of the three authors of this book, Dennis LaBare.

I have known Dennis for a number of years—can't remember how we met, other than somehow I became one of his wide circle of friends in the wingshooting community. I have hunted with him and behind his big belton setters, and a more dedicated dog guy doesn't exist—and I know a lot of them.

But he didn't get there all at once, and his experience pretty much crystallizes that of thousands of other late comers: The bird-hunting bug bites them; they hunt with someone who has a good dog; they get a pup; they expect more from the pup than he can deliver; the frustration grows . . . but so does experience, and hunter and dog learn from each other and become good at the game. That's part of the story as told by Dennis, his good friend and mentor Bill Horn, and Dennis's wife Stacy. They were helpers and observers, watching the change to Dennis and the canine star of this book, an English setter named Commander who, for 15½ years was the center of Dennis's grouse hunting world.

But there is more to it than that, for these wonderful dogs, because they occupy a unique place in our world, one not filled by careers or finances or spouses or children. In her section of this book, Stacy LaBare describes Commander as a "lifetime dog," and so he was. Like so many others, he became the dog by which all those to follow were and are compared and judged. We forget the faults, the seemingly endless learning curve, the frustrating behavior in the field that seeks to ruin an autumn afternoon. Instead, we remember only the good, the skill and tenacity, the companionship and love, and we say to ourselves, *There will never be another like him.*

In this book, the pearls of advice given to Dennis by Bill Horn are jewels for any dog person to add to their collection; you can learn a lot about training a grouse and woodcock dog by reading his section alone.

But if you did, you'd be cheating yourself, because this is a book about the evolution of a sporting life, a life well lived—and how so much of what we do, we do for the dogs. And that's because their lives are spent—every moment of every day—doing for us.

STEVE SMITH
Editor Emeritus
The Pointing Dog Journal

ACKNOWLEDGMENTS

T HE AUTHORS, with deepest gratitude, acknowledge our parents and other adult mentors of "The Greatest Generation" who saw to it that when it was time to enter The Great American Outdoors with a gun, a dog, a fishing rod, a camera, or a backpack, it was so. A special thanks to Lawrence Knorr and the staff at Sunbury Press who recognized that the story of a unique part of this special generation known as "The Baby Boomers" was worthy of the telling.

PRELUDE

H E'S BEEN GONE just over four months as I write this. While the tears don't come as often, they still do. Worldly admonitions tell me time marches on, heals all wounds, and that we should look ahead. But that's not how it's working. As the weeks and months pass, I find myself moving inexorably backward.

It's a search for something I've known, experienced, but did not etch to clear recall. I should have written it down, keeping a diary as friends advised. But I didn't have the discipline, I guess. Perhaps that's not completely fair to me. It's not like I didn't have an excuse. Middle age, divorce, a new business to build. Who wouldn't fall into the "tyranny of the urgent" that so easily crowds out the important?

But even after I retired and had the time, I had an excuse.

There was the drive to get all my dogs time afield, their care, my insistence on pursuing sometimes dizzying amounts of volunteer work—and looking after two homes. But now, that's all it is—an excuse. I seem to be measuring my life by how long Puppy's been gone, remembering when he first came home, the special moments that come to me at quiet times, or when I glance at his photos on the wall.

The journey backward has more shadow than sunlight. It takes place at odd moments. Riding in the car to anywhere, particularly to hunt—walking mindlessly on a woods road while a dog is coursing the adjacent cover, but mostly on the edges of night and sleep, just before dark.

From somewhere inside, I'm back to the same beginning, more than any other place.

It is a mid-November morning after an overnight tempest. My friend Bill and I are walking in a snowy stream valley, tall with hemlocks. The mid-morning sun struggles to find its way to the forest floor. Large white clouds, their undersides dark, scuttle overhead, the day trying to clear. The large Hemlocks, well-spaced, stand sentinel to the little brook and nearby young forest, all backed and filled by open spaces of mountain laurel, winterberry, and small pines. This enchanting place Bill had named Lower Twin Creeks, now all blanketed in an other-worldly soft, white powder, the Hemlocks hanging heavy with snow.

Bill is walking somewhere to my right. Approximation is all that's necessary. Bill has been my field partner for five seasons now. We know each other's pace and way of making cover. My young Setter has pointed some of these very scarce, uber-jumpy grouse in his second full season, but we are still yet to close the deal. Now, he is somewhere between us, generally working back and forth through the snow-laden cover, his bell tinkling alternately clearly, then softly, then mostly muffled. Following these moments, there will be a rapid ringing as he stops to clear a snowball from a foot and shake himself, the snow-choked bell ringer suddenly freed again to make its rising and falling music.

At a moment when snow-hung trees and thick, laurel most separates us, there is silence. Then I hear Bill's muffled call "Point!" and I work the obstacles as best I can. But before I see him, there is a shot, and as Bill comes into view, he quickly explains that Puppy had been pointing and that my approach might have helped to put up the grouse, but he just kept swinging through a snow-covered bough, so he's not sure. As I gaze at the opening in the trees, we both see a few fine, soft bits of downy feathers drifting back, settling, turning, and winking in the sun. It all happens quite fast. As I'm walking around to a clearer view of the bird's flight, I see my young Setter just turning toward us with the grouse in his mouth, its head and tail hanging limply at either side, walking calmly toward me through the snow.

On one knee, I accept his offering. This moment comes to me, and it is those times leading up to it and all that followed that I'm trying to remember. They flash in pieces or roll out as long pantomimes, playing out often at the edge of slumber, a moving tapestry. The tale of my life that can't be told without telling his. Endearment called him Puppy.

The remembering of the years come and gone, the moments, the savoring, the ups and downs of life, each night it comes back to me. A small clearing in the snowy wood, the sun breaking through the clouds, and a dog, as white as the world so new to him, carries his first grouse to me. A moment frozen in time, Puppy, Bill, and me, forever young among the old, old Hemlocks.

Upper Tract, West Virginia
January 2009

· Part I ·
DENNIS

CULTURE

I was born in the suburbs of a large American city to parents who lived the Great Depression, fought the Second World War, and came home to build the peace under threat of nuclear holocaust. Like many of their contemporaries, my parents derived from more rural parts of the country and had moved to larger cities out of necessity during the Depression just before the war years. The eventual war-time industrial mobilization and the work it offered was salvation for many, including my people. That time presented more than ample opportunity to find employment where hard work and clear thinking, if not necessarily a college education—offered a way up the economic ladder. Surely in many cases, it was as much about survival as anything else.

Along with the values of such hard work and discipline, many carried with them a love for the farms, forests, and brooks they left behind and the hunting and fishing they remembered. Many fathers of that time tried to convey, some with more vigor than others, the joys of such field sports, all learned from their fathers and uncles in a simpler time. Mine was one of them.

In a modest house in the suburbs, I gradually became aware of hunting and fishing, if not to a pretty simple and limited extent. There was a pair of shotguns in an upstairs closet, including an old side by side with a short stock I was sure once belonged to my smallish paternal grandfather. I would learn later that this would be called a "hardware store" gun. It had no brand name or manufacturer markings on it, just "Proof tested 20 ga" and "Patented Apr 20, 1915." I've been told it's likely a Stevens. But as a boy, none of this was important, and actually, still isn't.

There was an old musket-looking gun with the single pull-back hammer and a metal butt-plate. It had a small swing-over breach where a twelve-gauge shell would be loaded and a long barrel that looked to be the same diameter from end to end, unlike the tapering form of the twenty-gauge. It, too, had a very short stock. I would learn later that this was called a "trade gun," an old musket, in this case of French origins. It had a shotgun barrel and, as I was told later, used in trade with Native Americans or other early peoples on this continent and likely others. How it found its way to my family remains a mystery.

When my parents weren't looking, I would fool around with these guns, picking them up clumsily as a small boy, sighting down the barrels, opening the breaches, closing them, and then pulling the triggers as I imagined some unremembered target. My father also had a twenty-two-caliber rifle, bought in the late 1930s, a Savage Model 5 bolt-action gun. I would marvel at that, going through some of the same motions with it. On days off, he told me that he shot rats with it at the Baltimore City dump. Just try that now.

There were fishing rods, too, in dull aluminum tubes containing brown-grainy fly rods out of early fiberglass. My father's, made from Herter's blanks, were built by a gifted machinist friend of his I would meet much later, a guy, as I remember him, who had no complete fingers on either hand. I would see my father take his tackle to go trout fishing, his leather-trimmed wicker creel and green canvas duffle by the front door, with rubber hip boots laying over the pile. Dad and Mr. Chet, an old friend of both my dad and my dad's father, would, from time to time in the spring, travel an hour or so to the nearest western mountains to fish Hunting Creek for trout. The fishing tackle took on comfortable normality, seeing it as I did casually stacked about for these trips. But it was the guns that retained a certain mysterious quality, for I never remember them being used during my childhood or early adolescent years. The only story I recall of hunting was when Mr. Chet's name came up. Dad would tell me how Mr. Chet could shoot a double on "pa'tridges," taking two birds out of the air with both in flight at the same time. I could tell dad marveled at this, but never did I hear him mention a desire to duplicate the act or pursue that sort of hunting. I remember seeing a picture of a 1953 Chevy sedan in my grandparent's Massachusetts dooryard with a deer taken in

Maine on the roof carrier, and that is all the connection I had to my father's quiet and very modest history of hunting. That white-tailed deer was taken with a borrowed gun, but who's? I would later hear some stories that made clear his simple hunting adventures from his childhood days on one or more uncle's farms in his native central Massachusetts. They went about like this.

My father, his younger sister, and their parents lived in the densely built little Connecticut River town of Willimansett, Massachusetts. It was essentially a mill town that had declined as the industrial revolution had petered out, and the Great Depression had settled in. By this time, many of my forebears had already migrated to the towns that had developed an industrial employment base in the late 1800s and early 1900s. However, their or their immediate ancestor's lives were spent on or near the lands not far from these towns. By this time, work was very scarce there, witness, after my father's high school graduation in 1936, the hunt for his first job was knocking on shop doors in nearby Holyoke and taking the first offer. Twelve dollars a week at a grocery and meat market, he handed his mother ten of it each payday. Despite these economic disadvantages, there was still some time to get outdoors to hunt.

Some of my father's uncles had farms out beyond the edge of town, in the vicinity of the now well-known Quabbin Reservoir. To those farms, some now underwater, they would travel with shotguns to pursue Gray Squirrels, or maybe in summer, catch Hornpouts from the pond. It was typical of what people of limited means could do: Some sport, and just importantly, something to eat. Uncle Dolph, one of the uncles, the story goes, fancied a few cats on his farm—more than a few, as it turned out. He even named them with mostly common human names. A couple of dozen or more roamed the farm freely at any one time, and they had their way with whatever they could kill to eat. The menace of feral cats to local wildlife, especially their Gray Squirrel quarry, was not lost on my father and grandfather. On each hunt, they unlimbered liberally on the feline populace. Their activities, while unknown to Uncle Dolph, would be noted indirectly to my dad and his father when, upon returning to hunt at a later date, they would be met with Uncle Dolph's missing cat report variously naming "Tom and Joe," perhaps some others, he "hadn't seen in a while." Dad and grandpa never let on.

While I was aware of this sort of simple hunting, the mention of other game to my dad, like deer, rendered only a passing remark that his father had hunted them all his life in central Massachusetts and never saw one. Also lacking in any of my memories of my dad's comments or stories were things like bird dogs or nicer shotguns, or sporting literature, or gun clubs. In adding it all up, at some point, I realized my family was, to put it generously, not very well off, Depression or not. At this late date, that my upbringing did not include the passing of anything one might now call classic, vintage, historical, or of enduring value, comes as no surprise. It was pretty basic stuff. We did have a subscription to Outdoor Life in our home and, was likely, for my father, a small luxury that allowed him the chance to hunt and fish vicariously via the likes of Jack O'Connor or Joe Brooks. For me, that magazine was a portal through which I would slowly produce generational vitalization, however modest, in keeping the outdoor sporting trust in my family and taking it a little further ahead.

My father's family found its way out of central Massachusetts in what was likely not an unusual scenario during those difficult times of the Great Depression. My grandfather, who worked for Westinghouse, then in nearby Chicopee Falls, Massachusetts, was, in 1938, asked by the company to move south with it to Baltimore. His condition for moving was that the company would offer to my father and his eleven-month younger sister a job. With all parties agreed, the move was made. It was the Depression—it was that simple. If you had a job, you didn't fool around with it—if you were offered one, you took it. That sort of thinking was a symbol of the times illustrated to me many years later when I considered my father and a friend's father, who had long careers with their respective companies, but similar in only that way. Indulge me a little story.

I was an undergraduate at the University of Maine, during which time I became friendly with a fellow named Andy. Andy was a graduate student seeking an M.B.A. It would turn out to be, and remains, a wonderful, now life-long friendship. As Andy and I became better acquainted, I learned of his family's fascinating history emanating from a line of sea captains out of the square-rigger sailing days in Searsport, Maine. I also learned that Andy was born and raised near Philadelphia. It seems Andy's father aspired to study electrical engineering. He earned a B.S. and an M.S. in the discipline at M.I.T.—no small accomplishment. All this was taking him away from down east Maine. It turns out Andy's father spent his entire career—all forty-two years of it—at the same company—just like my dad. While some might argue that "it's different now," that people hop from job to job these days—which is indeed true, I'm convinced there was something else that went on with the Greatest Generation. Both Andy's dad and mine grew up in the horrific times of the Great Depression, and a job—any job, was treasured. So, in the case of Andy's dad, a guy with credentials to envy and who surely could have written his own ticket in the booming post war years chose instead to stay with his company. I believe this sort of loyalty was driven by something much deeper.

During Andy's working life—and he was no slouch, either—a civil engineering degree from Princeton underpinning his M.B.A.—I witnessed more of his father's thinking. At one point, Andy had looked seriously into the idea of buying a small construction/engineering business, something for which both his superb education and work experience had well-prepared him—only to be chided and scolded by his father that "he had a good job, why would you leave it?" The Depression begot just that kind of thinking—and for many, regardless of station or education, it never went away. The reader may safely assume that this philosophy of thoughtful no-nonsense was the underpinning of my upbringing and has been an important influence on my adult life.

An important note in the generational transfer of outdoor sporting traditions, or perhaps any pursuit of interest involving parents and children, is the way it's done. In my case, I will always sense that my father, likely without realizing it, conveyed to my brother and me his enjoyment of the field sports in what I would call a "non-intensive" way. That is to say, I believe he just drew aside a curtain or just opened a door a bit, and we were left to push on through if what we saw struck our fancy. This may have been on purpose, or just as likely, a consequence of his own more casual but sustained interest in things hunting and fishing. One thing does stand out: I never heard him and my mother argue about his going to the field, and I believe this at least kept conscious or sub-conscious negative overtones from seeping into his son's feelings about pursuing our outdoor interests. I suspect there's a lesson in there for anyone with children who would like to see their kids take up their outdoor pursuits—don't over-do the intro.

———

Our neighborhood in the suburb where my parents settled and where I grew up was a modest move-up community for folks of modest means who are working in the booming post-war era. It's not the first place they lived since they had married in '42. My folks had occupied a series of apartments in, and closer to, the City. My father was drafted the following year. Surviving the Italian Campaign, he comes back to work at Westinghouse where he was guaranteed a job if—he lived. That my father survived the war at all, in retrospect, seems a miracle itself.

By what I will always believe was a quirk of fate, my father had learned to type in high school. While on training maneuvers not far from my former home in Oregon, the troop trucks stopped, and the world changed for my family. With everyone lined up in the early morning hours of an all-night ride, an officer came down the line asking, "who can type?" My father dutifully raised his hand and was taken off to be an administrator of some sort with the Special Troops of the 91st Infantry Division. Shipped out initially to Algiers, he entered the combat of the Italian Campaign by way of the Anzio invasion.

As history has revealed, he was stuck on a troopship with many of his fellows as the Allies became bogged down by a very aggressive Nazi maneuver that only forestalled the ultimate Allied sweep up Italy's boot and the liberation of Rome. As my dad told me, the commanding general, Mark Clark, executed a very aggressive war supposed to be only an occupying front for German General Edwin Rommel. The idea of this was the hope of keeping Rommel's attention on Italy and off Fortress Europe's western front of France and the expected invasion there. My father felt it was way too aggressive and very deadly. "Everyone I knew was killed," I recall my dad saying explicitly in one of his rare pronouncements on his experience there. He was also commenting that his being in the rear was the difference between life and death. He has started just as an ordinary infantryman. Knowing how to type was a life and death difference. I was told to take typing in the eighth grade—and I did.

The subdivision in which our home was located was one of cookie-cutter Cape Cod-style houses. Ten grand a pop, most with two dormers on the front, a few without. It's $1500 more for the dormers—no small sum in those days—but we have them. They all have a front porch, concrete, with a wrought iron railing, and with one to a few steps of the same construction, leading straight to a sidewalk, all the same distance—from each other, from the sidewalk, and the street. The year: 1951.

Nobody had a driveway in our neighborhood. The Fords, Chevys, Studebakers, and even an Edsel or two, lined the perfectly uniform curbs. Our tricycles, cowboy hats and holsters, eight-foot redwood picnic tables, metal lawn chairs and chaise lounges with the thick plastic cushions, and the barbeque grills—would eventually fill the backyards that in the early days, looked pretty empty.

Like me, the hedges that some neighbors planted grew up over the years, adding a sense of order to the previously wide open, barren-like suburban landscape. The friendly neighbors had trimmed gaps, even little archways in these hedges, so we kids could go back and forth at will. It's that kind of place. In later years, some of our neighbors paved driveways in the narrow side yards, a sign of modest prosperity and promotion on the job. My father was in management for a few years, but we were not the first with a driveway. Since my mom didn't work, they watched their money. Life in the Cold War was solid, simple, and my folks, who grew up not all that far from the bottom of the ladder, were feeling pretty fortunate. But the real or perceived "security" of America being a superpower with "only the Russians" to worry about, having a decent job and a home, was punctuated regularly with geo-political and cultural events that reminded us we lived in a rapidly changing world. Sputnik, the satellite Russia launched successfully, created the idea we were behind in the space race as a matter of national pride and also created the fear that the Communists, along with having a nuclear arsenal big enough to kill us all, might secure space as a platform to endanger us further. John Kennedy's exhortation to the nation that we "land a man on the moon and return him safely to earth in this decade" challenged and focused us all and made us feel we, as a country, were doing something about the Russians. The invasion at the Bay of Pigs, a military and political disaster, reminded us we were not invincible. The expansion of the Vietnam War worried many parents that their children might be sent off to war—as many were—just as they had been less than a generation ago. Kennedy's assassination, Elvis "The Pelvis," the rise of the counterculture with "free love hippies" and their drugs— plenty was going on while my brother and I had pretty blissful childhoods underneath the umbrella of it all.

Our TV was black & white, as they all were then, the screen round but for the framed edges making the sides straight, speaker below, all of it in a small living room space-eating piece of wooden furniture. TV was still quite young. We watched *Lassie, The Lone Ranger*, and since World War II was not that long ago, *Navy Log* and *Combat* (with Vic Morrow!), and *Walt Disney*—of course. What I didn't know is that my family was just one of the millions in post-war America in similar circumstances, and my four-year older brother and I were known as "baby boomers."

———

The first hunting I can remember that made me curious enough to wonder about was in 1966. My mother had purchased my father as a gift a Winchester Model 94 lever gun in the traditional 30-30 Winchester caliber. I'd guessed it was the same model my father borrowed in previous years to hunt in Maine. That fall, my dad went off to the Eastern Shore of Maryland on a deer hunt with some work friends. This must have really grabbed me, for the following year, I would refinish the stock and add a scope to dad's Model 5 Savage .22, and that summer, be allowed to carry it—unloaded at first—on what would amount to a walk in the woods, ostensibly a ground hog hunt. Looking back, it was really an exercise in gun safety. Could I carry it pointed properly at all times? The answer to all those questions must have been correct, for following instructions sternly given, when he let me load it, I tested the safety, and it went off. Notice of my properly carrying the gun pointed away from my dad—and the repair of the safety was, shall we say, immediate. That fall, I was able to join the Catonsville Scouters Rifle & Pistol Club near my suburban home, to learn to shoot formally. I would travel to Maine that same fall and accompany my dad on my first real hunt—for deer—and it was on that trip I would have a startling introduction to a bird that would play a prominent role in my future.

CONNECTING BACK

Given my family's origins in New England, and with plenty of relatives remaining, it was never any wonder to me that for vacations, we traveled principally to Maine. It did not occur to me as a youngster that Maine was known, for many years, by virtue of the moniker on its automobile license plate as "Vacationland." Indeed, it was for me, but I was oblivious to the commercial aspect of all this. To me, Maine was my vacationland when I went back to visit my mother's side with an occasional stop in Massachusetts to see my paternal grandparents. It seemed like my father was not all that keen on swinging out into central Massachusetts to visit his folks as that took us west out of the main highway corridors and increased the overall travel time to get to Maine—where he really wanted to be. In all this, the "generational clock" of time removal from my family's rural origins was, in a certain fashion, being turned back for me, even if that was never the intent.

As a small boy, the anticipation and adventure of packing the car and heading north were big doings. What I didn't know then, of course, was that my parents had made this trip many times. My awareness of what we were doing, and as I would learn, was that there had been many arduous trips with a crying, screaming baby who never slept for the entire trip. My folks would often drive "straight through," as we came to call it, and that insufferable baby was me. This was well before superhighways, the trip being many hours longer than it would be today.

So, the idea of heading to Maine and it being a certain return to the rural origins was not a conscious thing to me; it was just "the way it was." Of course, in the process of this, I acquired my father's delight in fishing, being near the lake, and wandering in the woods, all of this in abundance and of high quality. It was an affection come by honestly and naturally, with no coercion by anyone.

I can still remember those clear, impossibly calm mornings at the edge of Big Lake when we would be staying at my aunt and uncle's camps, the small business they ran seasonally renting cottages to fishermen and vacationers. After a couple of weeks, the rhythms of idyllic camp life had become second nature. But this would be the morning for my family to go back to Baltimore—and in my memory, it was always like that—the sun creeping up over Hardwood Island a half-mile out across from the camps, the lake surface like a mirror. And of course, there would be loons, singing what had to be their farewell song to me. These loons . . . they became so emblematic of that place and my memories of it. I even had a way of trying to converse with them during my later Summer-long stays. I would accomplish this by cupping both my hands and blowing across my thumbs. These same loons, impossibly shy, retiring, and the essence of wild things would, in later years, become astonishingly tame, taking bass from my hand at the gunwales of my Grand Lake canoe and earning nicknames from the fisherman they robbed of their catch.

My uncle, wearing his red and black buffalo-checked wool shirt, would be cooking the breakfast he always prepared for us on that last morning. The meal would be pancakes on his two-gas burner-covering black, cast-iron griddle. These mornings, in my memory, were usually cool. After all, it was lakeside and even in July, enough to want a small fire in the wood stove. The aroma of griddle cakes mixed with the faint perfume of a birchwood fire, with all of us in the knotty pine-finished camp to gather around the table one last time. It had a happy and a sad feeling to it all at once. Happy, for it captured all that enchanting place had become to me, but sad, for it signified that our annual vacation, plenty of time for all the terms of endearment to fully obtain, again—had come to an end for another year.

This was my pre-adolescent and adolescent life, one that I was quite unknowingly lucky to have. While it might be easy to think it was specially destined for me and how it would become so important and valuable to me, I have to think there's a larger thing going on here. I will always think that any youngster exposed to nature and natural things would become similarly enamored with that reality. It was just my luck that I was the guy in that particular piece of the great outdoors. So, when the big news came to my ears in early 1967, I was all primed and ready. The groundwork had been laid, the die cast.

With my brother's graduation from high school that June and the anticipated expenses of his college education in plain view, my mother had gone back to work. She had continued to work at the Westinghouse defense operations while my father was overseas during World War II but had quit sometime after hostilities had ended, anticipating starting a family. Like most families of the day, my mother stayed home with my brother and me while my father worked, creating a stable, healthy home life for us. But with the changes in boys growing up, and the need to finance my brother's college, the math dictated this change. But this left the question open about me. Long before the age of "latch key" kids, who let themselves in after school with both parents at work, the Summer of 1967 would have left me hanging in our suburban neighborhood. Our community was safe and clean by any standard, but looking back, I can see my parent's wisdom. The unrest of the 1960s was well underway, and with it, things like illicit drugs were becoming more commonplace. To them, there just seemed to be the potential for problems. Idle months during summer, to them, just looked like trouble, and so the call to Maine was made.

When I heard the news of my parent's plans for my Summer, I was jubilant. For me, I had not become part of any neighborhood culture or group, to the extent that its pull would have been irresistible, so when I was told I'd be headed to Maine for the Summer . . . heck, even as I write this now, I can still feel that certain sense of exhilaration that attended the news. Summer in Maine! What could be better? Reflecting on this, I recognize that "going to summer camp" is pretty common, especially to those born a bit further up the socio-economic ladder. While I had done a stint or two at such a place in previous years, this was incomparably better.

My version of summer camp (on Big Lake!!) was a bit more bohemian in that I was a "working" kid. I did chores around the camps, chores quite essential to the operation of the seasonal enterprise. There were boats to clean, outboard motors to repair, wood to split and haul, camps to clean, people to greet—I did things to help our guests, and it just seemed natural. It never dawned on me that I gained valuable interpersonal skills and a work ethic, all this built on the strict manners and politeness drilled into me by my parents. But there was tons of fun, too. There was never a day when I didn't have a motorboat or motor-driven Grand Lake Canoe at my disposal to fish as far and wide as I cared on the 18,000-acre lake out front. There were guns to shoot in the gravel pit as an additional diversion and for learning safety at my uncle's hand. My experience there was a great combination of responsibility and fun, and I count it among my very most important formative experiences.

The summer of 1967 would begin for me, what would become a boyhood romanticizing of a place and, in the end, a time that set much of the course of my life from those years forward. I would spend the summers of '67, '68, '69, and '71 at those same camps, on that same lake where we vacationed when I was a boy. The opportunities in the outdoors, the culture surrounding them, the feeling of it all. They put me in a place and a state of mind, I guess I was meant to be.

FIRST AWAKENING

Sports, fishing, and girls occupy the near completion of my sophomore year of high school. In fact, it must have been these other teenage influences that caused me to not spend the summer of '70 on the lake in Maine. In looking back, I wonder what I must have been thinking. Upon the completion of the school year, I would decide to play league fast-pitch softball that summer. I wasn't a bad athlete. Though I had completed the ninth grade elsewhere, when my mother transferred me to this small, private, four-year prep school, she had me start as a Freshman, so I am a little behind my contemporaries, except for driver's education. Starting fresh at the beginning, perhaps it assuages my sense of being out of place, but only a bit. I imagine that the teenage, not-quite-a-man desire for some kind of prowess was the underpinning of what now looks like a foolish decision to play ball and not go to Maine. But it turned out to be a smart move, if only by chance when my appendix burst in July, and I had immediate and world-class medical care minutes from home.

———

It's probably a Tuesday or Wednesday night in early spring of 1970, a school night, and after the obligatory homework and some TV, I've found my way to bed. The night is ordinary. Much later, I'm awakened to uncontrollable crying and sobbing from downstairs in the dark of night. There has been a phone call.

My mother's parents still live in Maine, where my mother was born and raised, and as they have done for several years following her father's retirement, her parents have just spent a portion of the just-past winter with us. The cape cod second floor is in knotty pine, finished by my father in the evenings after work. My room is at one end; guests use the other, separated by a standard but open door frame. At that other end, while visiting, were my grandparents. Their end is roomier and has big closets, and is closest to the stairway. Near the end of their stay in mid-March, my grandmother has had some tough nights in much pain, something that is not explained to me and that I do not understand on my own. Returning to Maine, she sees her doctors, is immediately admitted to the small-town hospital for heart tests. The phone call: My grandmother is dead, killed by a massive heart attack while waiting over night for the electro-cardiogram to be read by a doctor in distant Bangor. Such was the medical technology of the day and the distance to better care.

My mother is inconsolable, and we all try to rally around her as we hastily make plans to travel to Maine for Nan's funeral. It's a long ride that includes a lot of driving in the dark. I'm not sure when we leave toward week's end, but the ordinarily two-day ride takes quite a bit less. The little house in which my grandparents reside will be at the end of our trip. From the still un-green suburbs of March in Maryland to the snow patches and gray-dirty roadsides of downeast Maine, a world away but a haven for summer vacations, now it's a dull, depressing landscape, somehow fitting the errand at hand.

The small village of Milltown, Maine, is our destination for my grandmother's proceedings, and in that town lives Lloyd Clark, my mother's cousin. A tall, slender yet powerfully built woodsman, he is the Maine Warden service supervisor in this area. He has huge hands, and his nickname is "Big Paw." Years later, I would see a display in the lobby of L.L. Bean that showed the first Maine Game Warden class (1929)—Lloyd Clark was in it.

Over the years, Lloyd becomes friendly with the luminary of outdoor types in Maine and beyond, and his fame as a warden, guide, woodsman, and all-around sport has him rubbing up against the likes of baseball great Ted Williams, sportscaster Curt Gowdy, and a host of mostly Boston-based outdoors/sporting personalities. Despite all this, he's a regular guy and likes my dad. What I don't know when I arrive is that my visit for the funeral will include a stop in Lloyd's kitchen to, of all things, watch some TV. I have no recall what took me there.

The kitchen is in a classic, old wooden clapboard farm type house that sits along Route 1 in the small unincorporated village. It has an ell, a building attached to the house also attached to the barn, is also attached to . . . well, you get the idea. This allows folks to access all their buildings without having to go outside, the whole affair running lengthwise and perpendicular to the road out front. The woodpile, a place for the truck, shelter for the dogs—it's all there in the ell. In the kitchen is an old wood cooking stove in addition to the newer model that runs off bottled gas. The old stove sits on curving legs and leaves a visible space where an animal could lay quietly if it wanted. On this day, there is a dog. It's now Sunday, and in the afternoon, a favorite show of mine and my dad's is on, The American Sportsman. But on this date, it's different and special. Lloyd Clark is the star guide. The other star is the Setter under the stove. His name is Joe.

Just three years before, on that first deer hunt, we are on the family lands that my grandmother's forebears once owned. They since had passed to the Clark side, thanks in large part, to the Great Depression. Sold for taxes during the Depression, Lloyd had a job following his entering the Warden Service. While a modest 300 acres, in the beginning, the "Howard Lot" as it was known, Lloyd, to his credit, had continuously expanded his holdings over the decades to more than ten-fold the original acreage of the Howard Lot. This forested domain had stayed in the family, and we were hunting this country thanks to "Uncle Lloyd." I clearly remember one morning with my dad, walking down the Nash Lake road, my great uncle's 30-30 lever gun across my chest, some kind of bird roaring and hammering its way skyward from right between my boots, leaves flying, and me jumping like I'd seen a ghost. As I stood blinking in astonishment, Dad explained to me that it was a partridge or Ruffed Grouse. Today's TV show is all about Lloyd, NASCAR legend Cale Yarborough, and Joe, hunting grouse and woodcock in the classic coverts of downeast Maine with Curt Gowdy narrating.

———

I had graduated high school the previous June and was living at home while attending a junior college just blocks from the house. Meanwhile, my dad, looking at retirement in just eight years, he and my mom are pursuing a place to build a home some distance west of the suburbs, in farm country, more or less. They seem to want a place with a little breathing room, space for a garden, which will carry them into old age. This area is still largely agricultural in nature—corn and soybean fields, overgrown stream bottoms, and small wood lots. Many unpaved roads lead off the uneven, relatively narrow paved one along which my parent's lot is located. Visiting the lot's two or so acres is unremarkable. It's just un-mowed grassy pasture sloping gently away from the road, a small, weedy ravine several hundred feet to the rear, and then a quick up-hill immediately into a large farm field. I don't remember if it was corn or soybeans then. There's one house already built nearby. I recall how we sort of walked around the place, taking it all in, when suddenly there was a lot of commotion, wings flapping, and a lot of cackling-like noise down in the ravine. Some big birds with long tails—cock pheasants. I would get to know them before too long. It was the beginning of a slow introduction to the upland field sports when Maryland had some pretty good pheasant gunning, something that would not last. Another nearly two decades would go by before my luck would change to something beyond the pursuit of the declining big bird.

A CHANCE MEETING

I had finished college and graduate school and had finally quit working for the big defense contractor from which both my mom and dad had retired. I'd been working to develop my own business, was married for the second time, and continued to pursue a passion I'd developed for outdoors/volunteer activism starting around 1974 with a fisheries conservation group called Trout Unlimited. My high school friend and fishing pal, Bruce Craddock, had convinced me that a wonderful limestone spring creek, to which he'd introduced me in 1970, should be the subject of an intensive conservation effort. Resisting his coercion for a long time, I'd finally relented. Following a meeting in February 1988 with him and my TU mentor, Jim Gracie, all this just an attempt to blow Bruce off, I instead came away with a commitment to the project.

On this November day, I found myself at a very tony shooting club in eastern West Virginia. I'd gone there to meet a fellow who was purported to be highly connected to people and resources that would be necessary to advancing the spring creek project as Bruce and me, and now this fellow—seemed to envision. I was seeking him as president of the newly conceived initiative. His name was Bill Horn.

For his part, Bill had the juice as advertised, and his abilities and contacts, along with my own grass-roots experience, allowed the effort to fall into place quickly, and our all-volunteer initiative roared off the ground into prominence. Included in my budding friendship with Bill was a lovely female Ryman-type English Setter. At some point, after we'd worked together a while, Bill asked me if I'd ever done any grouse hunting. "Sort of," was all I could say, for I'd only tramped around the woods of western Maryland a bit in the company of others who knew little more about the enterprise than I did, which was essentially nothing.

Bill and I began hunting the mountains of Virginia and West Virginia some two to three hours west of his suburban D.C home just before the decade of the 1990s. He knew this country exceedingly well from the many years he'd explored it before our meeting. I was young and fit enough that I suppose Bill felt I could do these hunts. Bill, keeping himself in pretty good shape, seemed to have run short of contemporaries who had done the same. The middle-age bulge and coursing up and down the ridges of mountain grouse country were not a good fit for some of those old boys anymore. We soon became regulars, and in the process, I came to admire Bill's handsome blue belton Setter named Feathers. This little sweetheart trotted through the laurel hillsides, hardwood clear-cuts, and occasional alder and winterberry bottoms, stylishly pointing grouse and, in the damper places, the rarer woodcock. It was a revelation. I'd sort of "co-owned" a German Short Hair in the mid-seventies, which had gone with the then-girlfriend when we broke up, hunted a few times with a pal who had one that was just as bad, and kind of left it at that. But this was different. Here was a dog that knew its business and went about it with a self-assured sense of purpose and an unmistakable grace. And she was just adorable, her big brown eyes and easy-by-the-fire demeanor making it all so natural. Without realizing it, I was becoming smitten. Bill and I would follow Feathers together until her passing in the mid-1990s. It was a remarkable career that etched itself into both our souls.

My work with Bill on our stream initiative continued to grow along with our friendship, and in the course of things, we developed an idea to produce a sporting print as a fund and awareness builder for our project. This sort of thing has been used successfully on many conservation efforts like ours, so we wanted to give it a try. In the spring of 1993, Bill and I, along with artist Gordon Allen and his then-girlfriend, the editor/publisher of the best known and largest fly-fishing magazine, John Randolph (with whom I would become good friends), and a representative of Trout Unlimited, found ourselves at the Green Spring Valley Hunt Club. A very exclusive enclave of the well-bred and even better financed of Baltimore and environs, we are there thanks to a friend of mine who has sponsored us. The luncheon goes well; the deal is struck. The 275-copy edition of *Spring Creek Decision* would help our project build awareness and leave a lasting icon of our work and the priceless spring creek we were working to conserve.

On the way out to the parking lot to leave, I turned to Bill and told him simply that I think I might want to get a Setter, and would he be willing to help me? I'd been hunting with Bill now for several years, and for reasons I cannot identify, after no conversations I can recall with anyone else, I am somehow moved to begin this process. Feathers had made her mark. Bill replies that he would be happy to help me. For reasons I also cannot recall from that moment, I mention that things are a bit rocky at my house, and he shocks me with his own news that his wife is trying to get him out of his house—permanently. None of this is what anyone would call an opportune time to be talking about bringing a dog into the home. What could I have been thinking? I had not a clue about any of this except my desire to have a Setter. Looking back, I can only wonder what had possessed me. Truly, I knew nothing about dogs, only my observations of Bill and Feathers and some basics from my Shorthair experience. What possessed me to pursue such a course remains a mystery. In the process of a second divorce, there I was living several hours away from legitimate grouse cover, a new business demanding so much of my attention.

On top of all this was the often-crazy amounts of time the stream conservation work was demanding. A stable home for a fine dog, my circumstances could not in any way seem to be construed. But Bill had agreed to be a reference for me, along with Baltimore's most famous son of the outdoors, writer Lefty Kreh. They both knew a gentleman in West Virginia I could call to ask about a dog. It was explained to me previously by Bill that you just didn't go buy one of these unique Setters—they were "placed." This meant a process of referral, questions asked, and answers given that needed to be correct according to the owner or "placer" of these dogs. I would not understand until much later that, given my circumstances, how significant a role Bill and Lefty played in my getting a pup.

The details of my subsequent conversation with Walt Lesser are lost now, but I do recall being asked many questions and the type of queries meant to help someone with the dogs determine if a caller is someone who should have a dog. My referrals were very strong, for out of that conversation came the names and phone numbers of two of Walt's friends in the fancy of these Setters, Kay Pierce, also of West Virginia, and Dr. Max Sponseller, a veterinarian in Delaware. These two friendly folks—and good friends of Walt's—had used the services of Walt's prolific stud dog, Alder Run Leftik, so affectionately named for our mutual friend, Lefty. It was suggested without promise that there might yet be puppies from breedings conducted some time previously.

Somewhere I'd gotten the idea that I wanted a nicely ticked orange belton, and a male, for the practical reasons of not having to worry about dealing with female heat cycles. I'd seen a Setter in a magazine ad somewhere that had captured my fancy. Why Bill's lovely blue belton Feathers, over which I'd killed grouse and had seen work for several years, was not my inspiration, I'll never know. My first call was to Kay, who stated that she had a blue belton male who experienced an umbilical hernia. After a pleasant conversation, I politely thanked Kay and left it at that. A subsequent conversation with Bill revealed his opinion that I might be better served not pursing that pup as you expected a lot of vigorous physical activity from these dogs, and perhaps that condition, even after surgical correction, was not to be chanced. So, I called Dr. Sponseller and was delighted to learn he had one last pup he was willing to place, and it happened to be an orange belton male. What a lucky break. I asked Max if he could supply me with the pedigrees for the parents. He may have faxed them, he might have mailed them, I don't recall, but I immediately faxed them to Bill upon receipt. What I got in reply from Bill was simple and direct, a message left on my answering machine: "That's all you need to know, just go pick up the dog." It was three weeks before I could get to the good Dr.'s home, and, refusing a deposit, he had graciously held the pup for me. Again, I like to think that it was the strength of my referrals that carned me such credit, and what I can only guess were correct answers to some salient questions about my situation and my intentions for the dog.

COMING HOME

On a pleasant fall Sunday, my then-wife and I set out for Max's home in the Coastal Plain of Delaware, up and across the Chesapeake and Delaware Canal. It was new country to me, and its sandy flatness, farms, and hedgerows spelled quail. Max and his wife were gracious hosts as we looked over the puppy's dam, a beautifully and heavily marked orange belton. Two pups were remaining from the litter of nine, that included a female Max was keeping for himself. Her kennel mate was our guy, a sparkling white male. We were late in this puppy acquisition business, as it turned out—our "puppy" was a pretty good-sized youngster of five months, his scant markings just barely starting to show, his features not well-defined. How much of or how good a hunter he might be, were significant questions I'd never considered. The firmness of Bill's urging me to "just go pick up" this puppy buoyed me along on this quest, and now the subject of it all was right in front of me behind the chain-link fence. Max took the pup out of the kennel, already named as it turned out, so we could see him run. We headed out into his yard and back fields of his thirty or so acres. At that point, I wouldn't have known the first thing about what I was about to see. Would it have been his gait? . . . his speed, would he find a bird? He looked like a young dog running around, celebrating being out of the kennel, perhaps a bit nervous around strangers. But I do recall a particular moment. As the youngster raced around in Max's back field of Lespedeza near his pond, he tore right through a pretty good-sized covey of bobwhite quail that startled us and especially the pup. When the birds burst into flight, he stopped, obviously stunned, and a little bewildered with a bit of that village idiot look on his face. I didn't know what to think or say, but something in the back of my head whispered, "gee, I thought these things were supposed to point the birds." Max didn't seem too concerned, or at least he didn't let on, and so the romp continued. A couple of minutes later, I picked up a stick near a little beach on Max's pond and tossed it ahead. The pup grabbed it immediately. It brought it to me, and Max, apparently surprised by this retrieval, noted that was the first time he'd seem him be so focused on a retrieve and bringing it to a stranger, no less.

A bath, a four-hundred-dollar check, Max's signature on an ownership transfer document, and we were on our way, the pup deposited in the back of the Trooper in the large, foldable wire crate with the slide-out metal bottom pan we'd acquired during the three-week run-up to that day. I had no idea, of course, what was going to happen to me, what course I'd embarked upon with this new creature. I certainly had no clue how he could change my life or how he would change it to an extent I could never have imagined. I suppose this is not necessarily a unique perspective for any new dog owner. Anyone moving from not having a dog in the home to having one—any kind of dog—is in for some pretty significant changes. Driving back to Baltimore into a rapidly falling late October dusk, I couldn't know this was, truly, the first day of the rest of my life.

THE NEW ROAD AHEAD

When life is whizzing along, you make and implement decisions to get things done while simultaneously writing your history and that of any person or creature your direction affects. And so it was for Puppy and me. Getting him home, I now had to think about all the little things that had never crossed my mind. What would I feed him? Where would he sleep? What about this house breaking thing? We tried to keep our home pretty nice. In fact, every two weeks, we had a lovely lady named Suzie come in to clean it. How would she react to Puppy, and vice versa? The questions were rolled out in front of me in rapid succession. At least for the next seven months, he'd be eating what was called "puppy chow." The advice others had given me settled around going to a nice pet store and looking over the offerings.

The emotional element of being taken along by a salesperson who knows you want the "best" for your darling new charge must be in play here. So, upon entering the store, I was accosted by a nice woman who showed me the shelves of the various brands. She had a recommendation, of course, and it was not the least expensive on the shelf, that was for sure. But what she said made sense to me, the cost of it was what I felt was reasonable, and so off

I went with a forty-pound bag. I was lucky that Puppy liked the chow and had a pretty good appetite to boot. So, for the next seven months, Puppy ate his puppy chow. I might have changed flavors, but I don't think I changed brands. It never occurred to me that he might have gotten bored with the same food—it took a while to consume a forty-pound bag—but he didn't seem to mind. This was just the first of a lot of things about Puppy that had they been wild variables on each of the salient elements of home life, I would have been in big trouble. While I probably should have been more introspective and thoughtful about these things, what did I know? Thankfully, Puppy was very understanding and forgiving. Until one morning.

I was developing my business, and I needed to go out to meet with clients, visit job sites, etc., and didn't want to, nor did I think I could, safely leave Puppy at home. Of course, the solution was putting his crate in the back of the SUV and loading him up. Until then, I was in the habit of feeding Puppy in the morning, and this morning was no exception. My preparation for the day, including feeding Puppy, complete, I headed out for my appointment on the other side of town. Since the crate was below the top of the back seat in the cargo bay of the vehicle, I could not observe what my little friend was experiencing, and perhaps just as well. Everything seemed to be going fine until I cracked the window on my side, the fresh air then circulating the car's atmosphere. I then smelled the unmistakable aroma of what could only be described as cooked grain, like oatmeal or something similar. But I ignored it until I arrived at the office I was visiting and walked around to open the back compartment. Ahh, and there it was, Puppy's breakfast deposited in a neat pile, the form of the bits of kibble altered little from when he had wolfed them down an hour or so earlier. Along with this were copious amounts of drool in the metal pan of the crate. It was slippery, and he was having trouble standing up out of the mess. I felt so sorry for him, for while he gave me that baleful look of my having stuck him in an impossible situation, it somehow had just a little note on it of "you know damned well that if you were whipped around in the back of this thing, your cookies would be in a pile, too!"

But Puppy was a flexible guy, and he adapted quickly. I continued to want to travel with him, and my time away from home was growing as the business expanded. So, I persisted. Not wanting to rack up many miles on the SUV that I preferred to use on weekends for recreating, I bought a used sub-compact station wagon. Lining the back compartment with a piece of carpet, this became Puppy's private space, and he learned quickly how to make himself comfortable. English Setters are supposed to be number twenty-seven on the dog intelligence scale, but I don't think anyone told Puppy. He learned almost immediately that he could accomplish two things by laying down and curling up in the corner up against the back seat. First, the car sickness that afflicted him disappeared. Even better, the drooling that accompanied it, that made a mess of things in the metal crate and left him so thirsty was also a thing of the past. Oh, and I only fed him in the evening now, not a minor detail.

Puppy and I became regular traveling companions, one of several stupid things I took up but got away with because Puppy was so calm, clear-headed, and adaptable. When we'd leave home, I'd open the back hatch of the little wagon, and in he'd go. His collected nature was just another stroke of luck for me. He became so familiar with the sights, sounds, and feeling of our travels that he rarely got up to look around when we stopped at my various appointments. But he was keenly aware of where he was, anyway, evidenced by when we made the turn and hit the bump of the low curb into our home driveway. Then, he was up and ready to go into the house. He became so much a part of the routine that after some time if I had been riding and yakking on the cell phone about business, that when we would pull up to a light or a stop sign, and he happened to take that moment to stretch or move about to change his spot, he'd startle me by suddenly appearing in the rear-view mirror. Shame on me. I'd forgotten he was even back there.

My life at this time was one that could be described as frantic. My marriage had collapsed, I had a partner that had been involved with business and more, and that too had collapsed. So, I was living in my own house as a sort of stranger and with a new business to start. This lasted for about five months until I was there by myself. As it became more apparent that my wife's income was going, going, gone over that time, I became seized with an anxious awareness that I was in a do or die situation. Puppy was there for all of it. Thankfully, business picked up quickly, but I didn't relax. My days were routinely sixteen, even eighteen hours, often with full days over the weekend. Puppy and I went to the local water supply watershed to help with the stress after dinner in the evenings for a walk of three or so miles. I walked at a good clip while he tore around the bushes and the mowed areas on this gated road with wide grassy shoulders. On warm evenings, when we got to the dam, he'd take a dip and have a drink, do some business, and then back we'd go the other 1.6 miles to the wagon. I was hoping to control my weight with this program—Puppy sure was, running like the wind all the while, but not me. One day in speaking to a friend about this, he said bluntly, "you need to jog to get your exercise aerobic, then watch the weight fall off." He was correct. It also helped my stress level and stabilized my appetite. Also, a terrific farmstand right by its owner's garden was along the road to the watershed, and I improved my diet during this time, thanks to lots of fresh vegetables and fruit.

Puppy, meanwhile, was rapidly becoming a mature dog, his classic Ryman head with the low-set, long, variegated or "belton" ears, and prominent occipital was developing into a classic shape that said, "English Setter the way we are supposed to look." He was handsome and striking, with his pure white coat and scattered orange ticking, not a patch marking on this dog—a true snow belton, as George Bird Evans was wont to call Setters marked like Puppy. The regular exercise for a dog that was bred to be athletic sculpted his muscles that rippled, and, visible under his luxuriant coat, he cut a striking figure. Puppy was a canine anomaly, virtually unknown in a suburban setting like this. Those who would see him at the watershed, a place I shared with quite a few dog enthusiasts who appreciated its lack of traffic, open space, and water views, rarely failed to stop and ask me all about him. I was a proud owner while at the same time annoyed with the attention, as the encounters required me to tell the story of his breeding in an elementary way—every time. Best of all, he mostly liked people. While tending to approach adult men from the rear after the both of us had trotted by, often startling them, women were met from the side as we approached. He accepted their hand while avoiding the men's. But little children were his joy. Walking or in strollers, he'd go right up to them, and I, often running behind, would be trying to close the distance quickly, as sometimes I could see the consternation on a young mother's face. I needed to reassure her that Puppy was friendly and harmless. Parents who would have a dog of their own with them were the most amenable to his visits, but parents without dogs were usually guarded and warded Puppy away from their youngsters. Understandable. They weren't dog people. Could they possibly know what they were missing? After our romp and a quick shower, I'd head to my basement office for the remainder of the evening, Puppy following me right down the stairs and usually to his favorite spot.

That spot was his crate. Fallen into disuse when I bought the wagon, the crate that had served to contain him in the SUV now took on a different and equally important function. Since Puppy had house broken effortlessly and without a single accident while doing so, I consigned the crate to a place it stayed until we moved from the house nine years later.

My office was pretty crude but functional. In addition to a desk and shelves, I had a simple table about five by three feet. It was green metal with a rubber surface, a military surplus sort of thing, and I used it to roll out project plans for review and some simple drafting. But the crate was just too big to fit where I wanted it to go, right under the table. So, I found a couple of regular, solid, masonry bricks, standard red ones, and broke them in half. One of these pieces under each leg and the crate just fit. I put a small cotton bathroom-type rug in the metal pan, and there was Puppy's spot. Since I never closed the door, he used it as his cave, a place to hang out, for when he laid in there, he faced me at my desk, the table oriented at right angles to the direction I sat when I worked at my computer. He and I were partners now, and while he didn't add anything to my business per se, at least not yet, his constant company was a joy. As the business succeeded, it might have been easy to leave him in the back of the car after working hours while I caroused in a bar or something. It might have been that I could have left him at home and gone out or, if he might have stayed in the house while I was gone during the day, to be left in the evening, too. But he was my responsibility, my charge, and the idea that he was something to live around never dawned on me. Most of all, he was my friend, and I wasn't going to be leaving him like that. Several times each evening, he'd come over to my desk and ask me to take a break. He was a vocal dog and his sometimes-rhythmic yowling or guttural vocalizations, often both, were something to make you smile. He'd come over to the desk and take his muzzle, and flip my hand up off the computer keyboard. If you put it back down, he'd flip it up again. He was not to be denied. So, I'd push back and swivel on my chair and talk back to him, asking him what he wanted. This was often met with his walking toward the utility sink if he wanted a drink. Sometimes, he'd make me follow him upstairs to the door, so he could go out and do his business. He'd often take me up to the kitchen, stop in front of the fridge, and talk to me about that. "That" meant he wanted his slice of cheese or baloney that he knew resided in the deli drawer just for him.

But the most fun we had on those little breaks was when he would approach me close between my knees and then turn a little so that I could grab his tail. During his yard training, I'd taught him the two-blast whistle as a "go on" command to urge him forward if he was too close as we ran or if we were starting out. This he knew well and, in the house,, he made it his fun. With his tail in my hands, I would make a two-blast whistle with my mouth and picking up my feet. He would tow me across the floor on my wheeled office chair, going right into his crate as I let go of his tail. He'd then turn around in the crate, come out, yowling and talking with delight, all the while ready to do it again. For my part, I'd push straight back toward my desk, him following me right back and turning, waiting for me to take his tail again, and with another two blaster, we'd be off. It was a simple, maybe silly little routine, but oh, such sublime joy—just me and Puppy, best friends forever. These breaks would often come after having my face stuck on a computer screen for a very long time, and he somehow knew I needed a break. He was my partner!

If I had field work in a more rural area, Puppy and I would sometimes go together to work on project sites. What possessed me to take him to strange places that had hazards from barbed wire to abandoned wells, to deer he might have chased into a road, I will never know. While I was identifying plant life, analyzing soils, and hanging flagging to delineate wetland boundaries, among other things, he was sniffing and generally nosing around. If he wandered a bit too far off, once in a while, I'd try teaching him a lesson about it. I'd hide behind a tree just off a path in the woods. After a couple of minutes, he'd come down the path, turn off where I had slipped behind the tree, and walk right up to me. It amazed me that he could just do that. I guess a little of my scent was in the air, and his exquisite nose just took him to me. Later in life, I would see him do this under more demanding circumstances, and I would be even more amazed.

On my runs from office to job site, home, and all around town, Puppy would accompany me, and quite often, I would take him into client offices. This went over better in some places than others. Since he was a little nervous around strange men and surely a bit about strange places, this discomfort would reveal itself in some drool or foam accumulating in his jowls. I would often see this and usually get to wipe it with a paper towel before it found its way to an office worker's pant leg, but at times, I missed it. Some in the offices had a sense of humor about this, others, though subtly, less so. But we made friends in some of these offices, and when I stopped taking him around with me after a while, some folks would ask about him. I'd just tell them that he was quite comfortable luxuriating himself at home on my bed, keeping watch over the driveway, patiently awaiting my return.

LADIES' MAN

It was in the spring of 1994, as my business continued to expand rapidly, that I found myself going farther and farther away from home in the region, following the work where I found it, and having to deal with ever more government regulatory personnel who had authority over the land use changing activities in their respective jurisdictions. In the early 1990s, the State of Maryland had passed what was known as "enabling legislation" in the form of the Maryland Forest Conservation Act. By enabling, they meant that each local jurisdiction—county or city—was empowered to develop a set of regulations for the conservation of tree growth affected by land development. Since things like development, zoning, and other land use affairs were typically under local control, the Act was passed with such consent so that local affairs stayed local. For me, a consulting ecologist, this meant that every time I crossed a county line, there was a new set of rules. Pursuing business in every county in the region where I could find it, I needed to know the rules of the game, and often this meant calling on government officials in their offices to go over things, usually while looking at client plans on paper. One such jaunt took me to the offices of the Maryland National Capitol Parks and Planning Commission—Prince Georges, in their county seat of Upper Marlboro, Maryland. This is a county on the east side of Washington D.C., and with two beltways to negotiate, along with numerous primary and secondary roads thereafter, it was quite a drive. Since I had not been leaving Puppy at home by himself for inordinately long periods, on this day, I took him with me. For his part today, Puppy was keeping an eye on things from his headquarters in the back of the little Subaru wagon.

It was late in the morning, approaching noon, that I arrived in the offices of said government officials, and with several rolls of plans under my arm, I entered the low-rise office complex. Approaching the front desk, a pleasant middle-aged woman absorbs my query: "I'd like to speak with your reviewer-of-the-day, or duty person, I suppose. I have some questions about Forest Conservation." Eyeing me, she says, "just a moment, and I'll show you to Ms. Miller's cubicle. She'll be with you in a couple of minutes." Indeed, I am shown back into the bowels of the office that has many County employees working busily at their computer screens or murmuring over the tops of the carpet-covered acoustic dividers so common then and now. It's similar to pretty much all the offices I visit, remarkable only for its sameness.

As I sat, being variously curious or nosy, I happened to notice a diploma from the University of Maine for an M.S. degree in Forestry. Next to it is another, larger diploma, written in what I only guess to be Latin. I have no idea what it says, the name of the person to which it was granted, as with the one from Maine, while clearly the Ms. Miller in question, is entirely unknown to me. As I'm gazing at these and also taking in some of the rest of the cubicle—the potted plant, a Philodendron, I think, snaking over and around the bookshelves and such, the obligatory "Cubicle, Sweet Cubicle" sign pinned to the carpet of the acoustic divider, I suddenly realize "Ms. Miller" has arrived, startling me out of my curiosity tour.

After a quick introduction, I mention to this woman, just a few years younger than I, that I, too, attended the University of Maine for my undergraduate degree. After minimal small talk about this, I sense that Ms. Miller needs to address my questions and have me on my way. Her's is a popular destination of late, what, with the newly enacted regulations and all. My questions answered, for reasons I know not, I ask her if she's has a moment to meet my puppy, who is just outside the office door. Surprisingly, she says she does. Stacy, as she immediately became, visits Puppy at the lifted hatchback of the wagon. True to form with women, Puppy sits up on his haunches unperturbed while she makes over him, scratching his ears, and talking to him, cooing, and telling him he's beautiful, me all the while, proudly taking it in.

So it was that Puppy and I had made a new friend. Driving away, I was pleased with my visit and the aftermath. As this woman had once worked in the private sector and understood the value of time, she would be a valuable ally in serving my clients effectively in Prince George's County. Unknown to me then, she would figure significantly in my life later on. I also realized I never did learn what that other diploma was all about.

LESSONS AND RITUALS

When Puppy stopped traveling regularly with me, while I missed him, I felt better that he was safe and comfortable at home, and indeed, comfortable he was. I learned that Puppy was spending his days on my bed, snoozing. With passing time, Puppy showed himself to be a completely housebroken and trustworthy roommate. When he would hear me make the driveway late in the afternoon, he'd pop up and be waiting for me at the front door. I could never beat him there. There would always be the yowling and talking behind the door as I tried to balance an armload of plans and files while getting my key in the lock. Behind the door, the racket and foot stamping, showing his impatience with my getting the door unlocked, was building to a crescendo. When I got in there, the fun would start. He'd be wagging his head back and forth, vocalizing like crazy, even yelping and running around the "circle" of connecting doorway openings, foyer to the living room, to the dining room, to the kitchen, and back to the hall and the foyer. This would go on for a bit, often including some crouched down feigning of going one way or the other, jumping on the couch, all of it with high-pitched yelps thrown into the mix of yowls and guttural talking. It was a couple of minutes of "man, am I glad to see you" pandemonium. I never tried to stop it. This was the pure joy of being the bond between a dog and his man. He and I were together again, and was it sweet! The routines of life at home are memories now, but back then, they were warm, daily rituals, the everyday fabric that added order and security, certain predictability, that made life good. Little things come to mind so often in these now later days as I remember him. Sometimes in the morning, mindlessly going through my routines, I recall how when I would stand at the bathroom sink to shave or brush my teeth, Puppy would slip in behind me and lay right up against my legs. I had to remember he was there, or I risked a bad fall, coming close one morning after leaning over the sink and finishing my teeth, beginning to step back for my towel, and feeling my balance about to go, which without a quick reaction, would pitch me right into the toilet. A quick grab for a nearby towel rack saved me.

Another favorite ritual was the shower. The small master bath in that house had a hinged glass door on its shower stall, with a towel ring right outside it as it opened. Puppy would lay down on the bathmat while I was washing. Upon my rinse and turning off the shower, as I reached out the cracked-open stall door, I'd call simply, "O.K.," whereupon he'd haul himself up and jump on the bed, one side of which faced the bathroom door. That's all it took. He picked up on these rituals so quickly and easily did what he wanted to do most—stay close to his man. Ahhh . . . what a time it was!

By the time Puppy celebrated his first birthday, things were pretty well-ordered. By now also, it was time to move him from puppy chow to his adult food, what I hoped, in my simplistic view, would hold him for the foreseeable future, which was both longer and shorter than I could know. When I went to the pet shop to look for his adult food, I remembered something Max Sponseller had told me when I asked about Puppy's feeding at his place. Max, ever the vet, figured a dog knew when it was hungry and would eat when it was, so he had a continuous feed hopper sort of thing that maintained a steady supply of dry food. Along with a good supply of fresh water, the dogs were set. But Max had a different set up than I had with Puppy. Max's indoor/outdoor kennel arrangement didn't require any discipline when it came to the dog's leavings, but our life did. Since housebreaking was in order for us, a feeding schedule was vital so Puppy's relief rituals would become known and regular. Since we had a lot of regularity in our house, I decided to give Puppy the choice of his next menu. I noticed they had a good supply of small, sample size bags of several different and competing brands of dog food at the pet store. So, I grabbed all of them that applied to our circumstances. It was six or seven different kinds, and before his last bag of puppy chow ran out, I took all of the samples, emptied them in cereal bowls, and set them on the floor in a row by the utility sink where he ate and drank. I'd grabbed extra bags of each type so I could make my data a bit stronger. Sure enough, Puppy would tell me I would need to confirm my initial findings. At dinner time that evening, I offered him all the different brands and flavors, lined up, side by side, and stood back. Like the serious-minded fellow he was, he approached the bowls and sniffed each offering right down the row. With this review complete, he then selected what he wanted to eat—and emptied the bowl. In case he had a second choice, or if the sample he ate wasn't enough of a meal, I left the other samples in their bowls right where they were. He didn't return. But after a while, when I took the second sample bag of the brand he ate and emptied it into that same bowl, he was right back to the line-up and ate his second helping. He still never touched any other bowl. Case closed. I just threw the other samples away. Puppy's credentials as an epicure were pretty limited, but he knew what he wanted—and what he didn't. While things with Puppy were going well, you can't expect there not to be some bumps in the road. As I like to say, "most people's problems are self-inflicted," that would be true for me, too.

I had heard and to a limited extent had seen, that a dog's appetite for his steady diet of store-bought dry food can wax and wane a bit—we humans never being sure just what causes this to be so. In the logical human mind, boredom would seem to play a part, but just how bored, if at all, can a dog become? Such a situation arose with Puppy, and I thought I'd help him along a bit by making what I thought was a nice, juicy change in his diet. Canned dog food is a well-advertised product seen on an everyday basis. Supermarkets, pet and farm stores—everybody has it. When you open a can, its aroma comes over as pretty pleasant, particularly when you compare it to smelling the inside of a bag of dry dog food. So, with these seeming benefits in mind—chunks of meat, gravy, and a nice aroma, one evening, I decided to give Puppy the treat of a delicious, meaty dinner—in place of his dry food. He devoured it with relish, my estimate of his having a sufficient amount being two full cans of a popular brand. He seemed genuinely pleased with his good fortune, as did I.

Later that evening, after the pre-bedtime rituals, we turned in for the night, and all was well. With my non-stop schedule that included a lot of fieldwork walking through the woods and swamps evaluating land development proposals, I slept quite soundly. But on this night, sometime in the wee hours, I was awakened from deep sleep to Puppy moving about urgently. Unfortunately, my response to his being up did not register soon enough, for after things quieted down again, my speaking to him and encouraging him to lie down and go to sleep, a tell-tale aroma found its way to my nostrils. After a few minutes, I was wide awake and realized I had a very big mess on my hands. Poor Puppy! He had awakened with a start and had no time to warn me or help either of us and had lost his bowels all over our bedroom floor. Ugh! What I did not know, of course, was that in addition to sudden changes in a dog's diet that can upset their digestion, canned food was very high in water as part of its ingredients, so it had "gone right through," in a manner of speaking. The previous evening's deliciously savored meal was now an unsavory mess. Lesson learned.

Our days and nights became ordered in ways that then seemed normal and routine, but in looking back, they were not only indicators of just how special Puppy was to me, but also what a remarkable dog he was in every way, something somewhat lost on me then.

At night, when the lights went out in the downstairs office and the rest of the house, I would head to my bedroom with Puppy close at hand. During colder months, while I was in the bathroom washing up for the night, Puppy was lying lengthwise on the same spot I would soon occupy. I'd don my sleepwear, and when ready to lift the covers, I'd say to Puppy, "O.K., make room for me." It was amazing, as I recall it, for he'd get up, begin to walk a circle on the other side of the queen-size bed while I was laying down in the nice, warm spot he'd left me. As I settled, his circle was about complete, and he'd lay down with his back up against me, a wonderful warmth under and beside me that was not only conducive to quick slumber but was also very comforting in a homey, snug sort of way.

We'd first worked out his being up on the bed in a simple way. After turning in, the lights out, Puppy would come to the other side of the bed from where I lay and rest his jowls there, looking at me. It was clear he wanted to be close to me. So, the permission was granted, by merely saying, "C'mon up." He'd gracefully launch himself and settle in next to me, and off to dreamland, we'd go—together.

In warmer months, Puppy might start on the floor. Our house was old enough to be built before the days of central air conditioning as standard equipment, so this house, retrofitted many years later, had the misfortune to blow its cool air out of ducts on the wall near the floor, rather than ideally out of ceiling vents. Summer nights would find Puppy moving about from time to time . . . from my bed to his bed to the rug, to the tile floor in the bath near the duct, all to keep a comfortable temperature. Puppy knew what he liked and where to get it. But Puppy's uniqueness went even further. While many dogs, as I would come to know over the years, will sleep fitfully while it is dark, most of them begin to stir as dawn breaks, which can be pretty early at some times of the year. Not Puppy. If I was asleep, Puppy stayed put with me. Even on weekend mornings with dark, dreary rainy days outside, the long, slow dawn and on into late mornings I'd sleep, Puppy never stirred. But when I did, all I had to do was open my eyes or begin to stretch, and there would be a thump, thump, thumping from Puppy's tail pounding the bed and greeting me for the day. If I happened to be looking at him when I awoke, he keyed into my eyes, and when they opened, his tail would start. If I closed them to doze, his tail would stop, but opening my eyes again would commence his greeting. On many mornings, I would awake to Puppy's head on my pillow right next to me, his long, warm body snuggled against me. I knew he must have adjusted his position sometime in the night to be there in the morning, but I never knew it. But that was like him. Puppy had a way of fitting in quietly, seamlessly, effortlessly, wherever he needed—or wanted to be. It was endearingly sublime in every way. What was not to love?

Readers who own dogs may look owlishly at this story, suspicious that this guy and his dog are just having it too good, that I somehow missed all the trials and tribulations of dog ownership, especially the first-time owner's blues. Well, I did miss many, but not all of them. The worst of them were stupid things I did, like not paying attention, not being careful enough, couched mostly in my lack of experience.

It was April 1st, 1994. Now fully estranged and even dating some guy, my wife was moving out, and the moving crew was in the house hauling her things away. Since there was some stuff of hers in the basement and the door to those stairs was by the back-kitchen door, they had both the front and back exits of the house wide open for their convenience. In all the commotion, I hadn't noticed that

Puppy had slipped out the door and, with the still unfenced yard, had gone on tour and into the yards adjoining ours that fronted on a bustling street, rush hour or not. Absorbed in what was going on and having no idea that Puppy was gone, let alone how long, the phone suddenly rang amidst all the uproar. Picking it up, a neighbor I had never met informed me that Puppy and another dog were having quite a time of it chasing each other back and forth across the busy street and recognizing Puppy from having seen him walking with me in the neighborhood, wisely and kindly scooped him up and called. I was embarrassed, relieved, and began considering the terrifying prospect from which these nice people had saved Puppy—and me after hanging up. Puppy had managed to dodge a bullet—a car, actually, to the extent I'll never know, thanks to a neighbor across the back fence. It was an enormous understatement to call it stupidly careless oversight on my part.

I can still recall the admonition of an old acquaintance not long after that harrowing close call. I was in Chambersburg, looking after some matter of Greenway business when I ran into Paul Helm, up from Baltimore and working the roadside stretch of the spring on the Skelley Farm with his split cane fly rod. Me, with Puppy in tow, had come upon him for an unexpected and pleasant chat. Looking back, I realize that Paul, an old-school sporting gentleman, recognized that the fine-looking young Setter I had with me was special, and with a cautioning word, said flatly, "now all you have to do is keep him out from under a car"—little did he know. It was starkly obvious but very sage advice, which for me up until then, had been just dumb luck.

———

Our rituals continued to develop. In the mornings on rising, I'd let Puppy out in the front yard to do his business. In the beginning, I rigged up a twenty- or twenty-five-foot webbing-type leash of olive-drab cotton, a snap hook at one end. The other end, I'd tied to the Flowering Dogwood tree several feet from the front door. Since I typically let Puppy out when I was bleary-eyed and barely clad, I had driven a flat masonry nail into a hole in the white-painted brick wall. The hole left when I removed the small mailbox, replacing it with a larger Bacova Guild model on a handsome four by four post with a new lamp. This nail allowed me to reach out the crack of the storm door, grab it, and hook it to Puppy's collar while he was still in the door frame with me.

Turning him out, he was free to roam its radius while I ducked back inside to clear my head and get my mourning routine underway. After using this arrangement for a while, I abandoned the leash and began letting Puppy out in the unfenced yard, unrestrained. I don't remember what prompted this. Perhaps hanging out in the yard with Puppy over some time caused me to think he had found the limits of our yard himself and would not go any further. This was the case until one morning when I got distracted and forgot I'd put Puppy out and ran frantically to the door. Upon opening it, I didn't see him. As he'd gotten in the habit of just laying down on the stoop and waiting for me to return, sometimes he'd bump the aluminum storm, my thinking he did that on purpose, and that would signal me he was ready to come in. But this time, he was nowhere in sight as I opened the door. I panicked when I didn't see him anywhere. Running the fifty feet or so to the curb and glancing up and down the street and into the neighbor's yards, my fear grew, for I still could not see him, and calling his name did not bring him into sight. My heart was pounding now, and I ran to the intersection of our street and another, just one house lot away. On the other side of the fortunately quiet intersection, the early morning traffic gone now, was Puppy, nosing around the yard of the house on that corner. Checking for cars, I called and scolded him back to me. As I was bringing him back and past my immediate neighbor's sidewalk that ended at the curb, as did ours, my neighbor materialized there and, startling me, noted that Puppy often took that little tour and also enjoyed one of his property, too. I realized two things just then: My negligence could have easily cost me Puppy's life under a car, and my neighbor was speaking to me in friendly code that I needed to keep my charge out of his yard.

As I ponder the life Puppy and I shared from this now distant and hopefully higher hill of our experience together, some things have begun to distill. The rituals and terms of endearment that found their way into our lives created a new reality that I almost unknowingly began to acknowledge in my quieter moments. Sometimes when sleep came slowly, or I awakened on an easy Sunday morning, I would lie there stroking Puppy and thinking about "things." I would wonder, in those moments of sweet bliss, where life was going, and when Puppy and I were both older, what it would be like? I expected to outlive, Puppy, but there was no guarantee that I would. Contemplating the more likely idea that I would outlive him, I couldn't fathom the idea of being without him in that subconsciously panicked moment. More and more, I began to define my life in terms of his development, his age, his likely longevity, our cherished moments at home, our enchanting times in the woods when I watched him course the mountain ridges. I loved his perfect, white form, either right beside me or as he blinked in and out of the hardwoods and Laurel of his Appalachian homeland. We were now long past the point where nothing else would ever be the same. Our lot had been cast together.

THE EARLY FIELD

Puppy came into my life ostensibly to be a hunting dog. From my distance as an observer of my friend Bill and his lovely Feathers, I could only see that part of the relationship between a dog and his man. I was fortunate to be truly enjoying the life that Puppy and I had quickly built, and had it ever been nothing more than that, I probably would have been quite content.

But the genes this dog carried, as I'd come to understand, portended very great things, though I had little understanding at the time of just what that meant. My original interest was to have a nice gun dog like Feathers, so we would follow that line as planned.

George Delatush ran the English Department at High Point High School in distant Prince George's County, Maryland, but lived not far from my parents in still semi-rural southern Carroll County. His place was about fifteen acres of fields and gardens included a wonderful rambling wood plank building with all sorts of little rooms and compartments inside. Among the spaces provided with both a sheltering inside and an outside pen was one with a pretty good number of Bobwhite Quail he grew and sold. For starting a young bird dog, this was a very fine set up. Thankfully, George was quite enthused about the prospect of seeing Puppy, for half of his pedigree came from Walt Lesser's Alder Run kennel in Elkins, West Virginia. Turned out that George had a heavily marked blue belton male named Alder Run Dangerous Dan. How fortuitous. We were a certain brotherhood in all this. The advice and opportunities to work Puppy on George's place were numerous, even when George was away—and I didn't waste the opportunity.

On my first visit to George's, it was a very dry, sunny, blustery, and fairly cold day in late November of 1993. Puppy was now about six months old. As I drove up the long sloping driveway, I was quite taken by his place; it sat upon the top of a hill while picturesque farming country rolled out to the horizon. But the fairly stiff breezes this day didn't seem to offer very good conditions for doing what would become the opening round of Puppy's exposure to birds—getting him to point the quail we would be planting in the weeds and fence rows that divided up the gardens and fields of George's place.

Since Puppy and I were new to all of this, George, and his friend Fred Fisher, who also owned a lovely Alder Run blue belton female, thought it best just to keep things simple. To that end, George got a single quail from the pen and, trying to get out of the wind some, dropped the bird into a good-sized tangle of dense Honeysuckle on the downhill side of his sloping fields and quite near a corn patch that had been harvested earlier in the fall, leaving only some stubble. With the quail planted, we waited a few minutes for the scent to disperse and then released Dangerous Dan and Puppy to see what would happen. As expected, they both picked up a scent and pushed their noses into the Honeysuckle, tails wagging with great interest. While this single quail didn't have much time to leave much scent, and with the swirling wind not helping matters, both dogs continued to push and snort in the Honeysuckle. Then suddenly, Puppy pulled his muzzle out the tangle. With Dangerous Dan being a nine-year-old dog of some proven performance, those watching, including me, didn't put much in what Puppy had done by withdrawing, except to conclude without saying that, as a youngster, he could be expected to lose interest.

We continued to watch Dan work around in this small area of very thick, tangled vines, fully expecting him to establish point, or perhaps in the case of the limited scent and swirling wind to, and if however inadvertently, put the quail to flight. But that's not what happened. By chance, I glanced around as I began to wonder where Puppy had seemingly disappeared. About fifteen yards or so away and slightly behind where we were standing, there to my right was Puppy. Out in the middle of the barren corn patch, Puppy was locked up on point. To our astonishment, my youngster had slipped away, as had the quail, quite apparently, and had found this bird huddling among the thin leavings of corn stubble and was standing him solidly. It was now evident that the young prospect had quickly shown up the mature, experienced Dan, and under challenging conditions for any dog, let alone a youngster in his first training session. Of course, I was ecstatic, but even in my inexperience of that time, I sensed a certain caution, as this didn't look good for my new friend George or his dear Dan. I needn't have worried. George, duly impressed by Puppy, saw no problem.

Later sessions at George's with both George and Fred confirmed not only our early experience and the notion that we had an up-and-coming prospect, but the satisfaction of seeing him point quail after quail, each time, getting more intense and stylish. Flushing the bird meant firing a blank gun near Puppy, and he had no objection to this at all. George and Fred were quite taken by this, and me by their enthusiasm. I don't recall my exact thoughts, but it occurred to me that this is what was supposed to happen. What little I knew!

With Puppy's initial training having gone so well, the next thing that seemed to be in order was a preserve hunt, it having been explained to me that this was a pretty normal sequence of events in the development of a young dog. A little luck and planning had set this up well for the next step. Earlier in the fall, I'd attended a Trout Unlimited fundraising banquet, events I'd run myself in the 1980s, and at that event, won at auction, a couple of preserve hunts, the first I'd take being at a place in Cecil County, Maryland. Knowing George was a shooting man, I asked him and Dangerous Dan to join us, as it was a hunt for two. Besides, I wanted George to see how Puppy handled all this. So, on yet another windy, sunny, but snow-covered day, we traveled to the farm in question.

The hunt consisted of eight pen-reared Chukar released in a field of corn stubble surrounded by woods, all of it covered by a few inches of fairly recent snowfall. But the big problem was the wind. As George and I started across the field in the direction of the cover, making our way between the rows of closely cut corn, the wind was almost howling at our backs at, I'd estimate, fifteen to twenty miles an hour—hardly what you'd want for a hunt. But Puppy, seemingly unperturbed by all this went flying down the corn rows as if frolicking in the snow, and for his pure whiteness, barely visible in it. But then something amazing happened. With Dan dutifully quartering the field as the wind blew vigorously from behind us, Puppy, seemingly not having much idea of what he was to do, ran to the end of the field some seventy-five or more yards in front of us. Puppy then turned and came running back toward us, but he didn't stop, just whistled right on by at full gallop. It did not occur to me at that moment that this was anything more than puppy-damn-foolishness, my youngster just airing out and frolicking all the while, but after a few seconds of being behind us, Georg turned and, speaking to me, gestured toward a brush line at the edge of the field and well to our rear. Turning all the way around, I had to look and look again, for the white snow, brilliant sunshine, and snow-white dog; even with the dark glasses I was wearing, it took a moment to sort it all out. But then, there he was, locked in a rigid point. As my jaw dropped and George and I started for Puppy to flush and kill the bird, George said something that still rings in my ears today: "Son, I think you've got yourself a bird dog."

HEART OF A HUNTER

I wish I could say that it was all glitter and glory for my new companion and up-and-coming bird dog who had shown me he had the right stuff. But the sternest test was still ahead.

By most knowledgeable sportsman's thinking, the Appalachian Ruffed Grouse is among if not the toughest game bird on earth to take. It's possessed of an uncanny ability to run from approaching dogs and hunters, sometimes turning and moving perpendicular to the direction of the wind. In mixed cover, often flying far into the branches of large evergreen trees, it will test the mettle of any dog and the hunter who seeks it. Some birds are so spooky, particularly if they are survivors of more than one season that they will fly away before they can be approached at all. The only evidence that they were even around will be a sensitive-nosed pointing dog pulling up on point with nothing there but the remaining scent. This is telling, for while you can often follow the logic of the cover to where the bird might have landed, likely much thicker cover, the chances are you will not see anything more but perhaps yet again, an unproductive point from your bird dog.

It was this caldron of demands and expectations upon which Puppy's pedigree rested. A pantheon of proven, talented grouse dogs preceded him up the family tree, and it was on the strength of his lineage I had acquired him and upon which Bill and I had rested our hopes. Bill's lovely Feathers was well into her old age when Puppy came on the scene, and I know Bill was hoping for a successor to lead us on future hunts. I was hoping.

Our earliest venture into the woods seeking grouse was with Feathers and Puppy and was the day after Christmas, 1994. A "clear, flawless sky, quiet 40-45", reads Bill's gunning diary for this date. He had chosen several coverts in reasonable proximity to each other to fill our day. We put Feathers to work in the Knob covert, but a good turn didn't move a bird. Moving to the Headstone Covert, we decided to give Puppy a solo turn. I walked up a bird, and in the process of following it up, Puppy had the bird bump off him, likely among the first two or three grouse in which he had ever been in proximity. Birds can be spooky; he's a beginner. Except for the scarcity of birds, none of this was a concern.

After lunch, we decided to put both dogs into the Upper Run covert, pretty good quality vegetation here as well and hoped for the best. It wasn't long before dear old Feathers began working her magic near a tangle of downed logs. Knowing this game very well, Bill began his approach to her, evaluating the shooting lanes and all the instinctively ingrained automatic thinking that attends the moment of truth. The grouse burst from the tangle and on his second shot, what turned out to be a gorgeous red ruff yearling cock bird was soon in hand.

Meanwhile, I was in the process of losing my mind and close to losing my dog. As it became apparent at the critical moment that Feathers was working game. As she stretched to point what would be the last grouse ever taken over her, my young charge was running around the whole enterprise as if he'd never smelled a bird of any kind or had the faintest idea what he was doing. Impatient and irritable, my too short memory forgot the fabulous work he had done in training and on the preserve. I was about to explode, and the thought, "why am I bothering with this disaster in progress." I couldn't understand how this highly bred dog who had started so well had suddenly put on a performance befitting the village idiot. I sat on a log despondent while Bill and Feathers, and rightly so, celebrated their excellent teamwork. Bill then turned to the matter of calming me down, no small task.

With the Upper Run covert pretty well worked out and the old girl showing signs of tiring, we headed for the vehicle. After a short break, we started into another nearby piece known to us as Double Woodcock. Bill, in his efforts to quiet me in my disappointment, insisted we take Puppy by himself into this covert that had not been hunted that day, at least by us, and see how he would do with fewer moving parts in his sphere, that is to say, with no other dogs. About three that afternoon, we began to penetrate Double Wood-cock, with Puppy coursing the cover quite nicely. Puppy slammed into a fine point in a matter of minutes, and with the imperative to put this bird on the ground, Bill and I began our approach choreo-graphed from nearly five years of hunting together regularly. But the grouse didn't care about possibly being the first point-flush-kill over Puppy or our ability in approaching the dog. That bird was out of there before any plans could formulate to a shot. Continu-ing, Bill walked up this bird that offered an easy shot, but he held his fire in hopes of following it up for Puppy to point. Sure enough, a couple of hundred yards on, Puppy's bell went silent, and we found him holding nicely. But this grouse did not get stupid on the flight into where it now listened to our approach, and when it flushed far enough out and with enough cover between us that all we could do was listen, we knew our day was finished. I whistled Puppy around and turned to head out of the covert. As Bill and I came into an opening to walk alongside each other, guns broken for the day, he looked over and spoke to me in words that echo to this moment—"you satisfied now?" I knew what he meant top to bottom. That afternoon in the Upper Run cover was not one of my best moments, and I deserved what he said and the way he said it.

I was lucky to have a gunning friend like Bill. In fact, over all the years, there's been no one like him. His insight to me, Puppy, and what I was experiencing, his calm demeanor built on a decade and a half with his dear Feathers allowed him to know what this day was about before it even happened. Bill was and remained in a unique position to observe with understanding and context, the unfolding of my experience with Puppy for the duration of most of his hunting career, something I could not begin to fathom from the view I had. That's why Puppy's story now becomes Bill's to tell. For me, this story is a coming of age that had I been a young fellow when all this good fortune befell me, would have seemed more as it should be. I was fated to a late start. But the boy-man had it work out, just in the nick of time.

My family's 1953 Chevy sedan, complete with my father's deer from Maine.

Allied forces took the town of Pisa, Italy in September, 1944. My dad (far left), his commanding officer, and another buddy, decided a tour to the top of the famous leaning tower was in order. The others pictured are unknown civilians from the town.

Even in a brutal war, occasionally there is time for a little R&R. Here my dad (right) and a buddy, enjoy a gondola ride in Venice.

My dad's principal non-clerical job was driving for his commanding officers.

A Boomer Cowboy: My brother on his birthday, 1952. It never occurred to us we were just lucky.

Best Friends Forever. My growing-up neighbor, Mark (left). The hedges and all else that ordered our lives were there for us. Nobody's mother worked in those days.

A brave new world came in through this box.

Simple times with simple joys: Little did we know.

Early lessons, 1957. I still tie with that vice, a Thompson Model B. My brother (foreground) remains an indifferent tier. The gooseneck lamp is yet a prized possession.

My brother, vacation 1951. He and I found ourselves with fly rods in hand at a very early age—decades before it became fashionable.

Hoeing Pa's Maine garden, 1957. My brother and I got to dig for our New England roots.

Lloyd Clark's legend extended to everything outdoors. Here, his English Pointer named Spot, feeds a White-tailed fawn. This photo, taken by Lloyd himself, is believed to be from an issue of *Fur, Fish & Game*, circa 1942.

The only known photo of Puppy as a puppy, and at six weeks of age. True Snow Beltons have no markings when they are born and remain so for many weeks. (Photo courtesy Anne & Max Sponseller.)

The begotten – partially formed: Cokesbury's Commander as a youngster of four months. English Setter conformation can take two to three years to fully mature. (Photo courtesy Anne & Max Sponseller.)

Ryman-type setter head confirmation at maturation. The classic occipital, square muzzle, low-set ears. Puppy had it all.

Alder Run Leftik, Commander's sire, in the glory of a woodcock point. Walt Lesser's most prolific stud dog, he passed into legend November, 1999. He was named to honor our mutual friend, Lefty Kreh. Note the classically conformed head structure of maturity. (Photo courtesy Walt Lesser.)

Cokesbury's Autumn Mist "Misty," Commander's dam. Puppy did not inherit her lovely orange markings. (Photo courtesy Anne & Max Sponseller.)

Puppy's enthusiasm and athleticism rarely resulted in spontaneous exhibits, but walking along the Falling Spring one day, he abruptly took flight, landing in the cool water and a lush growth of Water Speedwell, mid-channel.

A couple of Working Dogs. Puppy's beauty and sweetness won over a lot my clients. A good partner does that!

We were together. Middle age was good for both of us.

(Photo courtesy Bill Horn.)

Puppy and the Old Man. The kid showed us he had "The Right Stuff" from the get-go.

Puppy cleaned up his first formal hunt. Though pen-reared birds, he showed easily his nose was something extra special and under the worst of conditions. (Photo courtesy George Delatush.)

Bill's lovely Shadbush Feathers showed Puppy how it was done on a late December day. (Photo courtesy Bill Horn.)

Bill and his Princess, December 26, 1994. This handsome, red-phase cock fell to his girl's exquisite work. It was to be her last. (Photo courtesy Bill Horn.)

· Part II ·
BILL

BRINGING THE BOY ALONG

Dogs are children. Wrestling with both the canine and human forms has taught me that it takes a combination of love, patience, firmness, and consistency to succeed. Keeping them busy is essential, too, since idle hands, or paws, are the Devil's playthings. The owner or parent must also keep the lid on inevitable anger and frustration; training a bird dog—or kids—means training yourself. When these virtues interact with good genes, the results are memorable. It was my good fortune to go through the trials and tribulations with three outstanding children, a superb (but less than perfect) English Setter, and Brother LaBare's wonderful decade-plus relationship with Puppy. I earned plenty of gray hair along the way while creating layers of experiences and cherished memories.

No book or instruction manual prepares you to train a pointing dog puppy. Veteran advice helps the most but being in the ring is fundamentally different from sitting ringside. When a precious, insufferably cute 8-week-old puppy quickly transfers its allegiance to you and its education is in your hands, the pressure is on. Will it become the dog of your dreams—fire to hunt tempered by loving discipline, intense birdiness yielding memorable staunch points, and a loyal pooch that snoozes with its head in your lap after a great day in the grouse woods? Or will it be another out-of-control animal that races through the coverts, oblivious to you, blundering into every bird in the neighborhood? You have a shot at the former if you do your job, and even then, the answer won't be clear for at least a couple of years. The latter is assured if you drop the ball. Hence angst and anxiety torment the owner of a young pup.

This was my fate in the early 1980s. I stumbled into grouse hunting a few years earlier, got irredeemably hooked, and enjoyed a small taste of quality dog work. Searching for a grouse dog pup led me to George Bird Evans and his line of Old Hemlock Setters. He put his dogs on a pedestal and treated the few pups he bred as rare jewels to be carefully bestowed on selected acolytes. I didn't make the grade, having befriended a couple of down-to-earth West Virginia boys who had been quietly keeping alive the Ryman Setter bloodlines. They had declined to breed their Setters with Evans' dogs, and he took it as a great affront. I was guilty by association.

It became a blessing in disguise as I secured a Setter pup from George Hanson—one of the West Virginia "boys." The pedigree was long on Ryman dogs, Walt Lesser's (Hanson's friend) Alder Run dogs (also with lots of Ryman blood), Hanson's closely related Farmboy/Farmgirl lines, and a couple of Evans' older Old Hemlocks. We named the little female pup, white with one blue ear and one blue spot, "Feathers."

Dogeared dog training books occupied my nightstand. But the best advice came from Hanson. Besides the basics covered in the books, he admonished me never to pass up a chance to teach the dog something while in the woods, don't shoot birds she bumps into flight (or she will happily act like a flushing dog), be patient—dogs aren't perfect. Feathers showed lots of promise as a puppy, and her first points on preserve birds created "paternal" pride on par with my children's first steps or words. I Learned anew, though, that dogs are like children. Ages two and three feature willful adolescence and maddening inconsistency. One day the dog performs like a champ; the next, it runs around like a moron disregarding every command and showing no evidence it ever pointed a bird. After one of these moron episodes, halfway through Feathers' third year, I was despairing. George said to withhold judgment until her fourth season; Setters, at least Ryman-type dogs, apparently mature a bit later than some others. So, I ate a patience pill, put my head down, and continued training.

The following November, Hanson and I followed Feathers into West Virginia's Canaan Valley on a brooding, drooly day searching for woodcock and grouse. A few hours later, I penned an entry into my hunting journal: "I have a BIRD dog!" Miss Feathers had quartered the cover like a pro, pointed a dozen woodcock, nailed one grouse, and was all the dog any hunter could want. For the next eight years, she romped merrily through the woods doing wonderful work (usually) as my partner in pursuit of grouse and woodcock.

Like people, dogs have their ups and downs. An All-Star pitcher throws a shutout then gets beaten like a drum the next time out; pointing dogs are no different. Good ones earn and are entitled to a lot of latitude. After all, none of us have ever sniffed out a game bird. Some days scenting conditions are terrible, the birds are hyper jumpy, or the dog simply isn't feeling well. There were many times that Feathers did her job, and I couldn't hit the broad side of a barn with the shotgun. I once blew an easy shot on a perfectly pointed big cock grouse prompting a season-long slump during which I missed 21 more grouse over the dog's points. Thank God I wasn't wearing a shock collar, and Feathers had the control!

Time is our great enemy. It exerts a persistent unseen pressure because we know that time with our dogs is fleeting. Most can hunt effectively for no more than 12 years, and usually, there are only 5 or 6 prime years—when the dog has learned the game and has the physical tools to take on the tough mountain covers. Dennis and I were fortunate that Feathers's career ended almost precisely when Commander's began. Feathers's last grouse was taken on the first day I hunted with then young Commander—December 26, 1994. The day revealed the gap between an aging veteran dog, at the end of her career, and a young one full of piss and vinegar with little experience in the ways of ruffed grouse.

Winter served up a perfect day described in my journal as "Weather: clear flawless sky, quiet, 40-45 degrees." Brief tours of two small coverts produced only a single grouse that young Commander bumped. A place we called Upper Waites Run held birds earlier in the year, so we opted to give it a look putting down the dogs together. My notes tell the story: "Reaching the base of the hill, we turned to angle down through more choice cover. However, the thick deadfalls and exposed rock made for tough going, especially for my 12-and-a-half-year-old girl.

But steer Feathers near a grouse, and she knows how to handle them. A hundred feet below me to my right, she checked up, flagged, then crept into a point. I stumbled and ducked toward her, but she softened, tested the air, and began to work a running bird. Three more times, she pointed and flagged as she tracked the runner. On the fourth, she froze solid—low outstretched head, leaning forward with a rigid tail curling up slightly. Sixty feet in front of her was a tangle of downed logs. I wove through the cover, and drawing up on her left; the grouse exploded into flight. I was on it quickly, fired, and it fell with outstretched wings, a gorgeous redruff yearling cock with a solid chestnut tail band. Feathers, the old vet, had produced another wonderful Christmas gift." While this was happening, Commander was bumbling about showing no signs of birdiness, and Dennis told me he was worried sick that Commander was going to screw up and push out Feathers' grouse before she pinned it. Later he confessed much darker thoughts.

We put Feathers in her crate and headed downhill to another fine piece of streamside cover. Working solo, Commander was much more focused and showed his developing skills. He pointed two separate grouse and did a good job on some other jumpy birds prompting my written entry: "That was our last flush, but Dennis's faith was restored—Commander did well for a 19-month pup with a lot to learn about grouse birds."

A couple of weeks later, Feathers went under the knife for a very large splenetic tumor. She barely survived, lived another three years, but her bird hunting days were over. For Dennis and me, young Commander had to step up, and he did. At the end of January, Commander pointed three educated late-season grouse that offered us one fleeting chance that Dennis missed.

Next fall was Commander's second real season under the gun, and two-year-old dogs are notoriously difficult. They tend to range broadly, feeling their oats, and their points often don't last long—the dog checks up briefly then decides it can catch the bird itself. And in this age of slim wild bird numbers, most dogs are trained on pen-raised or preserve birds that are dumb as rocks and tolerate dogs pointing from only a few feet away. Wild birds are just that—wild. They do not tolerate such nonsense, especially hard-pressed Appalachian ruffs that have a keenly sensitive proximity fuse. A bona fide grouse dog better learn to point them from 50 feet away or more. Making the transition from the training field to the wild woods is difficult, and Commander suffered this fate.

Our first venture took us to West Virginia's high country—Canaan Valley and Mt. Storm. Conditions were less than hospitable—windy weather on day one and snow and wind on day two. Wind is a killer for pointing dogs; it whips away scent and makes wild birds extra sensitive. On day one, Commander found grouse and woodcock but bumped half a dozen birds. On day two, Commander blundered into more woodcock, finally pointed one but broke and chased out the bird as we walked in to shoot. Dennis needed an extra potent patience pill.

A week later, we were closer to home in the Virginia mountains finding nearly a dozen grouse for 19 flushes—excellent action by eastern standards. My journal characterized the day as "more steps in the education of a grouse dog and a wistfulness about Feathers' forced retirement." Mr. Commander tried hard. On grouse #2 he worked into a hard point by a streamside tangle and wouldn't budge even though the bird had run out. The Setter tried to relocate the runner but bumped into it for an out-of-range flush. The flustered dog then ran up another before settling down and registering a good point that offered us no shot. By day's end, Commander had pointed three grouse but had bumped or run up 10; my comment was, "oh for some steady dog work." However, the good ones learn from these experiences.

Eight days later, we were back in the same little mountain valley. A snowstorm dumped 10 inches of snow, turning the usually gray/

brown November woods into a white winter wonderland: "The cover was beaten down with saplings, jack pines, and viburnum all bent with heavy snow. The streamside hemlocks were posing for calendar pictures with snow-laden boughs glistening in the sun." The first grouse flushed from overhead, high up in a hemlock, giving Commander no chance for point and us no shot. Slogging downstream through the snow the dog bumped another from a pine thicket "but he redeemed himself in a hurry. Still among the hemlocks, the bell stopped, and I found Commander on a perfect point: leaning forward, head turned 90 degrees over his right shoulder, tail rigid and curling up. The grouse was apparently in a clump of snow bent small pines framed by the hemlocks. Dennis circled in from the left, and I stood ready to fire back up. The dog held, but before Dennis got clear, the bird erupted back over the dog, and I had a brief glimpse between the evergreens. Mounted the gun, swung, and fired. It felt like a good shot, but I couldn't tell. Dennis got free and looked over to see Commander bringing us the grouse! It was a fine yearling cock, and there were congratulations all around." A bird dog's first grouse over a point is a special occasion.

Some liken dog training to sculpting. I agree as it takes good raw material to produce a good dog. However, the great dogs demonstrate a level of learning and skills that cannot be taught. The late Datus Proper was a dyed in the wool pheasant hunter— when southern Pennsylvania and northern Maryland sported good populations of wily ringnecks. He had a German shorthair named Trooper, who was death on pheasants. The dog figured out that the best way to pin the runners was to scent a bird, circle wide, and come back to point the bird when it was between the hunters and the dog. Feathers did the same thing a few times on grouse; hunting for Dennis and me, she had circled and cut off a track star ruff, nailed it between us with a great point, and then we whiffed the shot. My old girl looked at us with disdain.

Commander was one of the smart ones. Another snowy day in the mountains had all the grouse up in the hemlocks and pines—8 of them, which we flushed 14 times. After our 7th overhead flush, the dog figured it out: "En route to the other side of the covert, Commander was below us and flushed another bird from some pines. This made an impression on the pooch. He went under a big fir, stopped, and looked up into the tree—it was classic!" I made a little sketch of it in my journal.

And like extremely intelligent humans, some bright dogs want little to do with their less gifted brethren. The smart ones seem to know that hunting with other pointing dogs without good noses or a sense of the birds will be extra difficult; that the less skilled dog will simply push out grouse and get in the way. Among people, we say, "they don't play with others." Commander showed these traits—probably a function of both his ability, awareness of his ability, and status as an "only child." For many years he was hunted alone until Dennis brought along a pair of other dogs late in Commander's life: Drifter and Taz. We followed a 10-year-old Commander and a young Drifter, another orange belton Ryman-type Setter, into a Massanutten Mountain cover in early February. Right away, it was plain that the senior dog was not pleased: "Our mistake was working the dogs together. Commander wants nothing to do with Drifter and reaches out too far. Drifter is more concerned with avoiding the older dog and hangs underfoot, showing little interest in hunting." Reaching out, Commander found some birds and registered three staunch points. But his reason for leaving Drifter in his tracks became evident when the young dog blundered onto point #3 and pushed out a pair of grouse that would have given us a fine chance for a double. I saw Commander exhibit the same imperious behavior in one of our finest West Virginia coverts: "Area 2." Taz was another young Setter that Dennis was trying to bring along with limited success. He put Taz down with Commander, hoping the junior dog might learn something by watching the old vet. It didn't work. Commander ranged far out to get away from the less birdwise Setter, and Taz just started running around out of control. When Dennis figured this out, Taz went back to the truck, and the old Commander reappeared, quartering nicely in range and nailing some tough grouse among the covert's legendary grapevine tangles.

Smart dogs, though, are up against smart birds. Nothing is tougher to pin than a hard-hunted eastern ruff, and the challenge borders on the impossible when conditions are poor. Quiet, damp days in the 40s are prized. The heavy air seems to hold scent, and dogs can wind birds from a distance. Grouse like to hunker down since they can hear their pursuers coming close; the birds rely on their camouflage and their speed if they need to get away. Cold, windy days, with biting dry air, are the opposite. Wind dissipates scent, air without humidity dries out a dog's nasal passages inhibiting its sense of smell. The noisy conditions cause the birds to flush wild at the slightest provocation. Area 2 in its prime could hold one to two dozen ruffs—a glut of birds by our Spartan standards. We hunted it on a very cold December day with a heavy NW wind feeling like an icepick. The covert was loaded with grouse hiding and feeding among tangles of grapevines laden with purple fruit. With 33 flushes, we got only three points from Commander: "Approaching the far grapes, we suddenly saw three grouse take wing from near Commander who never got a whiff. He was frustrated, realizing he wasn't smelling these ol' thunderwings that he kept running into. As I told Dennis, you rarely get good dog work when air is cold and dry, and it's unfair to blame the dog in these cases." Training the trainer never stops either.

Professionals insist that dogs are easier to train than owners. Many Setters, shorthairs, and Brittanies are shaped up nicely by pros, returned home, and promptly allowed to revert to old bad habits. The best trainers require the owner to attend school with their dogs so both can be taught simultaneously. And a big part of this training is the need to temper expectations and exhibit patience. Good quality dogs taken to preserves routinely register dozens of staunch points and locate every bird released that morning. Taken next to an Appalachian grouse covert, the dog might produce a couple of points and a couple of bumps in a hard day afield. Bringing preserve expectations to the grouse woods is a bad mistake. George Hanson always thought any dog that pointed more grouse than it bumped was a damn good one because the birds are so difficult to handle.

Like most of us, Dennis suffered early on from unrealistic expectations manifested in bouts of anger and misplaced impatience with Commander. Dogs are not automatons, and neither their progression nor performance can be measured on a linear scale. Too many variables are at play. Yet a set of good performances followed by the inevitable hiccup can cause an explosion of angst resulting in invective directed at the poor dog. This trap caught Dennis in 1996. Three of us—me, Dennis, and Joe Kelley—along with Commander and Joe's shorthair Reece—headed up into the "Two Shot" covert: a big expanse of little mountain streams, thick laurel and rhododendron, and regrowing clearcuts. It held a lot of birds then and produced 11 grouse for 16 flushes this day. The dogs started finding birds right away, and Commander registered a nice point on a fast-flying pair that eluded our shots. Reece then pointed another that Joe brought down. My journal notes, "unfortunately, Commander chose this moment to have a bad spell. He ran up a new grouse from a laurel tangle, ranged ahead, and pushed out another bird. Things were made worse by Reece promptly nailing grouse #6 that Joe collected quickly." Dennis simply lost it, angrily collared Commander, and started the long march back to the truck with the dog in tow. Hours later, Joe, Reece, and I returned to find Dennis still fuming muttering imprecations about the poor Setter. We talked him "off the ledge" by pressing a simple point: a pair of mistakes does not render a good dog worthless.

Anger management was beaten into my head by veteran dog men like Hanson and Lesser. A man should not vent his frustrations by abusing his dog and cannot if he wants the dog to succeed. Walt's first breeding was with Ryman's Blue Heather—a stylish dog turned into a "blinker" by a harsh trainer. Apparently, the dog suffered so much punishment for mistakes in the training field that she grew fearful of game birds and simply walked away from them—blinking. In the form of electric collars, modern technology makes it far too easy to abuse a young dog. Collars can be an effective tool if used judiciously, but some people electrocute their dogs and wonder why the dog loses its desires to hunt and becomes distant, if not surly. But regardless of collars, keeping frustration under control is necessary. Mistakes by a dog create an opportunity for correction and teaching—not abuse. That's easy to write yet hard to achieve. We invest so much effort, time, and hope in our bird dogs that when they fail to perform or stumble, it is difficult to reach into your soul to find the necessary patience.

I had been guilty of all these sins a decade earlier. Plus, I was going through a divorce with three kids while Commander was coming of age. Dennis was in the same boat, sans offspring, creating an extra source of anger, depression, and frustration. Keeping all of that under control and not venting it on our poor mute dogs became another imperative. Besides, our dogs were real anchors amidst domestic intranquility. The unflagging loyalty and love from a faithful pooch are never needed more than when your life is turned upside down, and you're emotionally adrift.

Full appreciation of a dog's ability creeps up on you. As we see our dogs every day and hunt them regularly, it is often difficult to discern progress. Incremental improvements become clear only over time. The visitor who hunts behind a dog at longer intervals often sees the improvements better than the owner. Almost all decent gun dogs will turn in an accolade earning performance or two. Steady repetition of good work and the occasional eye-popping point, over time, creates the realization that "I've got a good one here." Expectations become realistic as well. You watch other dogs and see that yours is pretty good. Plus, years in the woods deepen your understanding of exactly how hard it is for the dog, and you, to successfully hunt Appalachian grouse. In the late 90s, after a day moving nine grouse for 16 flushes and getting one good point from Commander, I wrote to myself, "today was one reminder of why each grouse is a trophy to be earned. Nothing else I know of requires everything to go right before you succeed in bringing one to hand. It's why after 20 years and some measure of expertise, the game hasn't lost its brilliant appeal." Feathers' apogee was at the end of her seventh season. We hunted a Virginia covert on top of Massanutten Mountain in the Shenandoah Valley. Found only five birds, but I took two over her points, including one that might have been her best point ever. She had disappeared into thick streamside cover and her little Swiss cowbell when silent.

Although nearby, I couldn't find her in the thicket until she took a small step to make the bell ring and let me know where she was. Turning back, I found her standing high and rigid by a big thorn laden deadfall. I closed, a big cock grouse thundered up, banking hard left showing a full spread tail fan. At the report, it collapsed from a stream of feathers. The following week, we closed the season in a West Virginia covert of steep ravines that held spooky late-season ruffs. Feathers pointed a dozen hyper birds that day marching through the cover like the veteran she had become, and I managed to shoot a pair. The most memorable was a point standing in a small stream; the grouse flushed off the bank and splashed down at my shot. There was a deep sense of satisfaction about how Feathers had turned out, and the remaining five years of her career were only icing on the cake.

I can't recall precisely when we knew Commander made the grade as a top-notch grouse dog, but a series of sterling outings in the late 90s persuaded me that Commander was special. He showed a great nose, a sense of the cover where grouse could be found, an ability to hunt wide but not too wide, and the uncanny skill to track running grouse and pin them. My summary of the 1998-99 season noted, "Commander has become a fine grouse dog." Dennis, too, realized slowly that his big orange belton was a good one. With that realization came the extra measure of patience that had been lacking, in the beginning, prompting a chicken or egg question: did Commander blossom because Dennis learned patience, or did Commander's development penetrate Brother LaBare's skull prompting more patience and understanding? Hard to say, but it was evident that they had learned from each other. And when Dennis was bringing along his next generation of Setters, the confident patience he exhibited was a marked difference and improvement over his early going with young Commander.

As a dog becomes a veteran performer, the concept of "success" begins to change. Early in a dog's career, the owner first wants the staunch points; shooting the bird is secondary. Once the dog demonstrates that it's a bona fide pointer, killing a bird over the point is the next requirement. So necessary that a lot of us clutched up hard and missed many makeable shots because we wanted it so bad. When these two stages are behind a hunter, success is more subtle. I found that the dog's great quality performance and good chances at pointed birds were the measure of a good day afield. Birds in the pocket were secondary. Yet when Feathers was gone, and I was hunting behind Commander or someone else's dog, birds in the vest became more important since the pleasure from the dog's work was diluted by the fact that it wasn't mine. Even so, good canine performance is always appreciated, and Commander offered plenty to appreciate. Another gray cool November day found us in the thick "Double Woodcock" covert—named such because when first found and hunted, I killed a pair of woodcock over Feathers' point. On this day, it held a bunch of jumpy grouse: "Commander did well on grouse that wouldn't hold. One did, and it tells a tale. We followed a pair of birds that had throbbed out of a jack pine/greenbrier tangle. Near the cover edge, the dog got birdy and worked into a hard point by a young hemlock copse. Dennis got in the open on the left; I was on the inside amidst pines, cedars, and thorny briers. We thought we had this bird. But it flushed directly over Commander screened from Dennis and took the one course where I could barely see it and was unable to shoot. They're amazing birds . . . We trudged back up the long lane, which seems longer when you're coming up with nothing in the vest, and reached the car in the gathering dusk."

Commander was now a mature veteran grouse dog. Hundreds of contacts with the birds, his inherent intelligence, persistent gentle training, some overdue patience from Dennis, and sensible expectations had come together. He and Commander were a potent team, and I was glad to come along for the ride. The prospect of woodcock flights had brought us back to Canaan Valley, but the longbills hadn't gotten the message. But we had no choice but to get out there and look. Unsuccessful forays into the southern Valley and nearby Dolly Sods prompted Dennis and me to try the northern Valley out the old Camp Seventy-One road. The area is crisscrossed by old railroad beds that a century ago carried millions of acres of board feet out of the Valley to sawmills in nearby Davis. Numbered logging camps dotted the Valley then, and we were going to try the alders, aspens, and hawthorns where #71 once stood. My journal recounts the events: "Reached the old camp area and turned back hoping we might find a bird or two on the drier upslopes above the old railbed. Just past the road fork, Commander swung out to the right and pointed in a group of 'thorns and young beeches. We bracketed the dog thinking woodcock. Suddenly a pair of grouse bored out 70 feet ahead, going hard, low and right. I had clear looks and shots—and missed. Disgusted, I tried to get a line on the pair. Off we went in pursuit, and only a hundred yards or so ahead, the upslope was full of downed trees. Commander ranged ahead, looking birdy, and slid into a fine point by the deadfalls. I got up on the right, Dennis covered the left, and the noisy beat of wings spelled another double flush. Grouse #1 went straight ahead, Dennis's gun fired, and the bird collapsed. #2 went hard left across the railbed, Dennis pivoted, the gun went off again, followed by an excited 'I got it, I got it!' Commander retrieved the first, and Dennis picked up the second. We admired a yearling cock and yearling hen, and congratulations were in order—fine dog work and fine shooting in a classic covert."

Sometimes I got to celebrate. Late January served up a sunny 40-degree day, and we were probing the "Cleavage" covert in Virginia's Shenandoah Mountains. The covert took its name from a pair of nearby hills doing a wonderful Grand Teton imitation—on a much smaller scale. Here the grouse held in thick laurel bottoms coursed by small foaming clear water rills. Part of the area had been logged about 15 years earlier, and the logging traces had once featured Forest Service signs "Seeded to Game Food." Now in a more politically correct era, the signs had changed to "Seeded to Wildlife Food." Working along the edge of the old clearcut, Commander locked up in the thick regrowth. We bracketed him, but the swirling breeze had confused the dog, and the grouse went out behind us. Marked its flight and set off after remembering an adage—one grouse leads to another: "the regrowth gave way to good laurel cover, and there was a thick piney swamp that looked prime. Commander carefully worked the shifting breeze and pointed into a laurel/greenbrier thicket. I swung around and walked toward the dog; Dennis was beyond him. Saw movement and a grouse ran out from 15 feet in front of the Setter, bursting into flight, offering a low "high house 3" try. Too fast with my first shot, the grouse folded and fell at the second report. At that, another grouse hammered out, catching Dennis flat-footed. Commander retrieved a fine yearling cock grouse with a solid black tail band, and our day was made."

Good dogs find ways to impress even old hands. Dennis and I closed the Twentieth Century in Five Flush, a Virginia mountain covert where Commander had once pointed a five-pack of grouse and LaBare's old humpback Browning 20 gauge misfired. We had only hunted its edges because the interior was a mass of thorns and thickets—piercing greenbriers, hooked multiflora rose, and wicked blackberry canes. I was insistent that we "circumnavigate" the place—go around the thorny center—and explore it thoroughly. An old logging trace led to the covert, and we parked in a tiny clearing back in the woods with evidence that some mountain girls were losing their virginity here. Parked, shouldered into our vests, assembled the guns and put the point collar on the Setter: "Walked out the logging trail with the thick stuff uphill on our left. Not far in, Commander ranged ahead to the left, and quickly the point tone sounded on the collar. Hustling up, we could see him on an intense point stretched out point. I got around to his right, Dennis took the left, and we moved in guns ready. As I neared the dog, he softened, took three or four steps to the left, and slowly swung his head in search of scent. It was as if there was a string from the grouse to Commander's nose as his head suddenly snapped to the right, and he froze. Twenty-five feet away under a small deadfall, I saw movement that blossomed into a hurtling grouse going out low to the right. Two guns fired simultaneously, and the grouse fell hard hit. Commander retrieved a handsome adult cock bird with glossy black/green ruffs, a solid black tail band, and a long 'yellow' tail. A fine last grouse for our first millennium."

Trusting a dog is often difficult. Some make it hard with incessant false points and false alarms. But grouse are so touchy that good dogs must be careful and false points are part of the game. Hunters who admonish or punish a dog for false points will never get a good grouse dog. A need for control is another hunter's problem. Even though a good dog may have pointed hundreds of birds, and you've never smelled a gamebird, the hunter wants to call the shots and disbelieves what the dog is telling him. I still kick myself for brain dead moments when I tried to call Feathers off birds she had scented and tried hard to find for me. Poor Commander had to put up with the same nonsense. At higher elevations, ice and snow drove us into the Shenandoah Valley, where we poked around a set of unknown covers. The first was an abandoned pasture growing into briers, cedars, honeysuckle, viburnum, and witch hazel surrounded by pines; a couple of spring seeps trickled through the thickets. It looked good, and some fresh grouse tracks in the thin crusty snow confirmed our optimism. There were grouse—and a bunch of rabbits. The Setter had shown birdiness a couple of times only to have a cottontail dart away. Nearing the back of the old pasture, Commander acted birdy again and slid into a soft point. I laughed, admonished him about bunnies, and a pair of grouse blew out. Oh well.

My last real grouse hunt with Commander was December 27, 2003. Dennis and I returned to Five Flush on a sunny 45-degree day. Intervening years revealed that the grouse liked the upper edge of the covert just below the ridge top that divided Virginia and West Virginia. Getting up there was a chore, and it took a lot of starch out of my then 53-year-old legs as well as aging Commander. But grouse are a narcotic for bird dogs and bird hunters—aches, pains, and wheezing lungs cure fast when a grouse sets the adrenalin flowing. Picking our way along the edge of the thickets, the Setter drifted down to the right, disappeared from view, and the collar sounded 'point.'

I Struggled downhill over downed timber and through clawing greenbrier. Still 50 yards from the Setter, two grouse hammered out—one went straight away on contour, and the second came uphill toward me all lit up by the morning sun. I would have had a good try, but it was between Dennis and me. I called 'grouse' to him, and he would have had a try, except I was in his line of fire! Damn birds."

The long slow decline of an aging bird dog is tough. Feathers was taken from me quickly as a hunter but enjoyed three years on the couch and taking the ride to the woods when I was hunting with Commander, Drifter, and Joe Kelley's shorthairs Reece and Remington.

Commander enjoyed a graceful retirement, and I still got to see him during hunting visits with Dennis and Stacy in Upper Tract. The Setter's timing was impeccable. Appalachian grouse numbers began to dwindle in the new millennium. Seasonal flush rates of 2 to 3 birds per hour shrunk to 0.5 per hour. A full hard day in apparently good cover might produce one or two grouse for three, maybe four flushes. Pulling the trigger on these survivors was difficult.

Plus, birds in full survivor mode make a good dog work damn near impossible. There weren't enough grouse for a good dog to learn the game and not enough to make hunting worthwhile even with a great dog. Reports of Commander's decline started in the summer of 2008, and by late that summer, he was gone.

In early August, Dennis called to report Commander's death, and we agreed to meet at the covert where we took his first grouse over a point 13 years earlier that coming November. We met, found the big hemlock where Commander and I were photographed with his grouse, buried his ashes, and said a few words of remembrance about a fine companion and hunter. Words were thick, throats tight, and eyes damp. A couple of miles up the road, we visited the old apple tree where Feathers rests, looking down on a glade that once held grouse and woodcock. Dennis and I missed our partners.

We hunted that afternoon with young Magic—one of Dennis' fine new Setters. Hours of effort produced only a couple of birds. My journal pronounced the hunting "dismal," making us "miss badly the 1980s with Feathers and Commander in the 1990s." They still live in our hearts and in their gentle innocent ways, taught us and gave us more than we ever could give them.

Puppy's first point/flush/kill, November 17, 1995. (Photo courtesy Bill Horn.)

November 8, 1997, a Red Letter Day. Puppy and his first grouse double over his point. It would not be his last.

By the time Puppy was into his third season, his prowess with grouse was well-established. Here with Allan Freemeyer (left).

With Commander, this became nearly routine for us.

Hunting or snuggling up, Puppy had it all down pat. Here with former Deputy Asst. Secretary of Interior, David Smith, in grouse camp, Canaan Valley.

Living in Puppy's Shadow. Ruffwood Chance and Rufwood Captain Magic with Bill in our West Virginia home.

· Part III ·
STACY

PUPPY FINDS HIS MOM

I met Commander and the man who would become my husband, on the same day in 1994. I was employed as an environmental planner/urban forester in the burbs surrounding Washington, D.C., Dennis was a very successful one-man environmental consulting show. Based out of his home, he delineated wetlands and developed forest conservation plans (among many other tasks) in the greater metro area for the folks building and developing things. He "got r'done" by multi-tasking to an alarming degree, I was to learn, while driving with his knees around the D.C. and Baltimore Beltways, his hands being occupied with a phone and whatever was for lunch. among other things. If it happened to be chicken nuggets, somehow, one or two would fly neatly over his shoulder to the beautiful English Setter in the back of the station wagon.

To make things challenging for environmental consultants, each county was free to create its own environmental regulations and pile them on top of federal or state laws. I could hardly keep track of it all myself, and I only had to worry about one county. So, my colleagues and I spent lots of time unraveling these restrictions on development and applying them to the plans and permit applications flying through our door. Part of that work involved being available for walk-in clients. We took turns being on call for this most unpleasant duty, and I was the Reviewer of the Day when Dennis and Commander came calling one spring day.

During our meeting, it became known that Dennis had a dog waiting for him in his car and that I was a dog lover without a dog. So, I was invited to leave my station (gladly) and go out to the parking lot to meet his pride and joy, Commander.

Commander was friendly with me immediately, and Dennis was a little surprised by that, saying that Commander was typically shy with new people. This was probably pure unadulterated bullshit because I later learned that Commander typically liked women, and Dennis found him to be a reliable chick magnet as well as a hunting companion. The truth was, Commander was friendliest, in descending order, children, women, and finally men. But so what? Commander liked me, and I liked him, so we had a happy first encounter. I was disappointed when Commander and Dennis had to leave to run his company. Being a government employee, I was about to take a good hour's lunch break and jog around a nearby pond. I fantasized how nice it would have been to have their companionship for the run.

Back in that period of my life, I ran almost every day. I felt sure that if I kept running, I could somehow leave my heavy heart behind me. So, I ran from the cubicle job, ran from the man, ran from the ticking biological clock. The result was a little bit more sanity and a tight little butt. As I became better acquainted with Den, he tended to doubt my sanity (still does) but told me he was impressed by the shape I was in (i.e., butt). I didn't mind the compliment. You might as well get something positive from all that torture. In the months after our initial meeting, we visited on the phone, sometimes related to work, sometimes not, and cultivated our friendship around our common interests. I was "attached" to another man at the time, but he was becoming increasingly burdensome and evil. It wasn't long before I realized what I had to do to have a bigger, better, and brighter life . . . perhaps a life with a wonderful man and a wonderful dog.

And so, I started the process of shaping a new life for myself, with new adventures and visiting new friends. The first time I visited Dennis' house in the Baltimore suburbs, I was sitting on the couch, and Den was at the dining room table, fooling with his slide projector and getting ready to educate me about his recent Maine fishing trip. Unsolicited, Commander quietly hopped up on the couch, cuddled close, and put his head in my lap. Like Commander was a "chick magnet" for Dennis; I believe I was a "dog magnet" to Commander. Or maybe there is another way to look at this: Commander himself could have been using Dennis to lure in friendly female friends. Yeah, I know, that would be anthropomor-phizing a dog (heaven forbid!!!!) . . . giving him too many powers of thought and reasoning. But, until you live with a remarkable dog, you wouldn't understand that almost anything is possible in the human-canine connection. Whatever the truth, I know that Commander and I had an immediate attraction. I didn't have that same attraction for Dennis until a little later . . . sorry, you had to find out this way, Sweetheart.

One time when Dennis and I shared a lazy afternoon, I asked about my new furry friend Commander, saying, "how's your dog?" Den thought I said, "How's your dad?" . . . and proceeded to share with me the recent trials and tribulations concerning his beloved and aging father. I could tell he appreciated the opportunity to talk about it with someone who cared. And I did care! But I felt like a real heel not asking about dad before dog. I listened with heartfelt compassion and waited an appropriate number of minutes to ask for the dog news. I don't think Den suspected my fickleness: true love breeds silliness, and I was in love with Commander. My love for Den would grow and blossom through the next several months as we carefully picked our way through past baggage and emotional minefields. But that Commander—he exuded love, and it was safe to love him back immediately.

When Dennis and I first shared a bed, Commander took his accustomed place next to his master and between us. Well! Even though I loved that dog, I also loved my new man, and I requested his (Commander's) removal to one side or the other, the foot of the bed or the floor. Den obliged, although I sensed a certain reluctance. After all, Commander had seen him through his rough times, and they were partners. As the years passed, Commander inched his way further into my heart and further onto the bed, until in his final years, he slept every night right between us. That was his safe place, and there was no objection from me then, except that my rear end hung out in the breeze.

Speaking of that, my tight rear end didn't last through the years, but the love of that dog did. Commander watched Dennis, and I fall in love, get married and carve out an interesting life for ourselves. Who's to say what the catalyst was? Was it the little butt, true love, or Commander's endorsement?

PEACE IN A BLUE ROOM

"Peace in a Blue Room" sounds like the title of a famous and wonderful painting, doesn't it? It is a famous and wonderful painting, but only in my memories. If I could put feelings behind "Peace in a Blue Room" onto canvas, I would indeed be a renowned artist because every human being would love that painting. They would look at the painting and feel a wave of relief and calm wash over them, transporting them from the stresses of their everyday lives.

Shortly after Dennis and I started our life together, we purchased a home on a hill in West Virginia. At the end of the climb up our narrow gravel driveway, we were rewarded with great views of rural life below and mountains in the distance. It was a peaceful place possessing that timeless quality one feels when looking out at the ocean or standing at the edge of some other great space. In more than the physical sense, we were indeed standing on the edge of a great space—a new adventure of unknown possibilities. We had decided to retire early, to spend one half of our year in West Virginia and the other half on a lake in Maine.

While Dennis took several months to close his business, I started moving our possessions to West Virginia, one load at a time. We would pack our utility trailer to the brim, max-out the space in the Blazer as well, leaving room for only the driver (me) and my traveling buddies, Commander and Taz. Our family had grown now to include a snappy little full-masked tri-colored Setter. We would wind our way to Upper Tract, unload our stuff, and settle down for a long weekend of whatever activities moved us.

Eventually, after all the stuff from Maryland found its way to West Virginia, I stayed there while Dennis sold and closed on the house in Maryland. That's when we took to sleeping in the Blue Room.

We called it the Blue Room because I had painted all the furniture a pretty blue, and it was on the cool shady side of the house, hushed by the nearby woods. Just walking in there, one felt the effects of the color: peace like the sky and the ocean on a beautiful calm day. My nights in the Blue Room coincided with a short period in my life when I was overwhelmed with peacefulness. I was free from worry and responsibility and in a little fantasy world. We can't possibly really live like that all the time, but it feels soooooooo good when we can have it for a week, a day, an hour. Commander, Taz, and I would pile on the bed, with the window to the wooded side of the property open so that the summer sounds were carried to us on the night breeze. We would fall asleep in a blanket of country quiet and only awaken with the gradual coming of daylight.

Dogs are peaceful creatures when they are not looking for dinner, grouse, or a game of fetch. When they lie down to sleep, they don't worry over the day's events or things that could have or should have happened in their lives. They just sleep. They just are. For this short summer season in the Blue Room, I was like them.

After years of conflicting events, I had been handed this temporary gift of peace to heal and start fresh. The person I lived with before meeting Dennis turned out to be a horrible choice for me. But I did not realize that for many years. We traveled the world together, and I learned lots of new things. We had many common hobbies and interests. I had a great paying job, a great place to live and play, and was able to save a ton of money. I called him my friend and trusted him completely, and I assumed he felt the same about me. He didn't. When I realized the errors in my thinking, I got more and more depressed, lost in a downward spiral of unhappiness and indecision.

How prophetic that he once told me that he was sorry he had to travel so much (yeah, right) and said, "maybe you need a dog."

Soon after that, when he was away again, for work and all his other selfish and sordid pursuits, I stood in the yard and spoke to his house, now emptied of myself and my worldly goods, "You are sooooo right, I do need a dog . . . instead of you."

And so, here I was . . . in the Blue Room sleeping with dogs . . . sleeping like a dog. Perhaps I had to go through all that heartache to arrive at this very point in time and to be able to truly appreciate it. If so, that's OK with me, for the end game was so worth it. God does indeed work in mysterious ways. Dennis and I and our ever-growing family of canines carved out a nice little existence from that summer forward. And although I was happy, I would not feel that overwhelming peace again until Commander's 15th year.

We had completed our annual springtime move to Maine in May, on his birthday, May 22nd. I was exhausted in mind and body from the transition, and I went upstairs, threw off my grubby clothes, and laid on the bed. Commander, my shadow in his old age, had followed me up there and hopped up on the bed, too. Together we fell asleep in the sun, letting the breeze from the open windows facing the lake wash away our cares. His fur was as soft as the breeze. How could I have known that this was his last trip to Maine? His last birthday? And this was our last trip together into a "Blue Room?" But this was another gift, another lesson for me. I never take naps! And here I was, having the best nap of my entire life. Thanks for the reminder, old buddy. Thanks for the birthday gift.

JUDGING DOGS BY THEIR COVERS

Commander was endearing, once you got to know him. But if you met him only in passing, you might not have been impressed. More than one friend or family member judged him too quickly, calling him a wimp, a wuss, or a creature lacking personality. Boy, were they wrong. Much like the adage "don't judge a book by its cover," Commander proved to be the most amazing dog once you spent time with him on his terms, or perhaps "turf" is a better choice of words when talking dogs.

When we judge a book by its cover, we may never open it, actually read it, and learn something wonderful in its pages. If we judge a person by our first impression, we may miss out on a life-long friend. And if we judge a dog by hasty and misguided human standards, we have missed the boat. Dogs aren't people—they are their own fascinating and complex species. And since they depend on humans for their well-being, we should be responsible enough to do right by them during this process, think outside the human box, and learn from them.

True, Commander was not one to run up to someone and slobber on them like they were a long-lost friend. Friendship is earned and cultivated. But he wouldn't ignore a human because they were chubby, grumpy, or had no cheese. He knew that these humans might be useful or loving to him, given a little time and patience. He also wasn't one to retrieve a ball or stick just because someone threw it. That would be a little ridiculous. He chose to retrieve something because we wanted it, such as a grouse fallen into the brush or a ball that no one else could find. How wonderful to bring to someone the thing they truly desire.

Over the years, I observed Commander's reluctance to act too doggy-eyed over people and their foolish games enough times to know that his behavior was by choice. He saved his true friendship for the people who loved him and needed him most: Dennis and me. When it came to other people, he studied them carefully and then decided whether to let them into his inner circle. My mom and dad are good examples.

My parents aren't dog people, but they tolerate well-behaved dogs, and they respect that I love dogs and always have. When I was a kid, I collected dog statues. Then, after lots of my pestering, they tried getting the family a real dog. The first two did not work out and were given away, amidst my many tears. Finally, the third one stuck, a sweet little Schnauzer that behaved herself without much training from us. Stubbs brightened our lives for several years, and we were all sad at her parting. I took the memory of her with me to college and beyond and waited impatiently for the day when I could have another dog. Pepper was that dog, a Husky-Shepherd mix of great athletic stamina. We went everywhere and did everything together. She graced my first marriage, and when that ended, I had Pepper to help me through the angst and loneliness. My parents understood this, and when they came to visit me during this time, we all stayed in a motel. Pepper, too. It was a big step for mom and dad to move their shoes and luggage so she could have a spot for her bowls and bed. A little later, I loved her enough to give her back to my ex-husband so she could live the rest of her life surrounded by his love and the Maine woods.

Finally, giving in to the fact that I have dogs rather than children in my life, my mom once threatened to do one of her famous needlework projects using the slogan "I didn't know all my grandchildren would be dogs!" Shucks, it's true, at least on my side of things. Thank goodness my brother provided a few grandkids. That took the pressure off me and left me free to raise dog-kids for the rest of my life. All kidding aside, including the cartoon-collage mom made of our garage doors opening and a herd of dogs running out, my parents have been very understanding. When Commander had to have a pricey major surgery in his 14th year, instead of asking why we didn't let him go," they sent a big check to help cover the bill. That was a very touching surprise, although their caring for him was not. They understood what a special fellow Commander was. He had won them over several years before.

It was summer, and a few years after Dennis and I had started our split-year life between Maine and West Virginia. My parents came out to Maine from Minnesota for a visit. Dennis was away, and I had to attend a meeting in New Hampshire, so they came along, as did the three dogs—Drifter, a big, white, orange-ticked Setter, was now in the mix. We had ourselves a fine getaway in the north woods. I put Taz and Drifter in crates in the back of the Explorer, and mom and Commander shared the backseat. I glanced back at them every so often, mostly to be sure mom was OK in dog world. I needn't have worried. As the miles drifted past, Commander inched closer to mom, and with his soft fur and quiet, retiring way, he won her over. Pretty soon, I heard the sweet voice I remembered from childhood, "that's a sweet, sweet doggie." Boy, don't you feel sorry for those wire-haired breeds? They must have to work extra hard for a good cuddle. Commander worked the same magic on my dad after a while, and I have a favorite photo of my parents and the C-man on the couch together. In comparison, my brother's dogs tend to avoid my parents and vice-versa.

Yes, Commander was a good friend to the people he liked. But his friends within the dog world were few. He lived up to his name in the world of dogs. As other dogs joined the household, Commander made it very clear that he was the top dog: the top dog to the people and the top dog of the couch, bed, and vehicle. No, he wouldn't ride in a crate, wear the e-collar for the invisible fence, or sleep on the floor. And that was that. When he was tired at night, he'd go into our bedroom, lie on the bed, and bark until we gave up and came to bed, too. He took such a dislike to his son, Max, that we had to give Max away at age 2 ½. Even in his old age, Commander was so fierce that he did not have to be physically able to kick dog-butt. His quick put-downs and sharp teeth were forbidding enough.

Speaking of poor Max, we requested he be returned to us after Commander's passing. It is interesting to note that I could not bear to write down my memories of Commander until Max came home. In a flash of white fur, Max brought a bit of Commander back to us in the flesh and made us think of all the good times. Only then could I think and write about my beloved Commander. Before that, I was keeping a lid on my thoughts and emotions. I couldn't even make myself go with Dennis and his hunting friend, Bill, to bury half of Commander's ashes at a special place in the

Virginia woods. My half of his ashes are still on the mantle . . . and will remain there.

Whether it was part of some bigger plan or not, Commander taught us things and made us better people. One thing I learned from his example, and struggle with still, is not to judge people too quickly or to dismiss them without really listening to what they have to say. It's easy to notice the people who are full of "pomp and circumstance" and miss the quiet and soft but interesting and strong person standing in their shadow. And sometimes, I'd just as soon ignore the folks who are a little "out there" when I compare their views of the world to mine. But what if I then miss the opportunity to learn something new about the world and myself or forfeit a grand and lasting friendship? What if we all, in our busy, harried lives, stopped chasing the same old sticks and judging books by their covers? It can't possibly hurt us to have a little more "dog sense."

THE THINKER

The way Commander hunted birds spoiled Dennis for all other dogs. In a way, it's too bad that all future dogs would never live up to Commander, Master of Upland Bird Hunting. On the other hand, Dennis, being a novice bird hunter when he got Commander, became one of the best bird hunters of all time. I truly believe this, and here's why. We would continue our Maine/ West Virginia lifestyle from 2002 through 2009 until we moved to our present home in Oregon in 2010. Commander, Taz, Chance, Drifter, and lastly Magic would hunt more than five hundred days under Dennis' gun during the five months of available seasons in both states. Without hesitation, I can say that no one alive hunted grouse and woodcock as much as Dennis and our lovely, talented Setters during those years. It was a time unmatched for dog and man. The work that Commander and Dennis did together was a beautiful symphony. Each needed the other for success and taught each what they needed to know about the sport as they went along. Commander's stellar instincts could only flourish because Dennis took him where he needed to go. Dennis's skills as a hunter could only develop because Commander took him where he needed to go. Often in the company with Dennis's closest hunting pal, Bill Horn, his exploits became the stuff of legend.

I never thought much about how smart Commander was until I read a veterinarian's evaluation of him during a visit to Virginia Tech Vet School for a detailed evaluation. Dr. Rogers wrote, "Commander is a very thoughtful dog." Being thoughtful implies that options for behavior are considered and weighed, and then a choice is made for what to do next. OK, that's logical for a human . . . but a dog? But here it was, in black and white, from a fully-fledged Veterinarian, Scholar, and Professor at a renowned Veterinarian School saying that our dog was thoughtful. And he had only known him for a few days. We had 15 years of observations to back that up.

Oh goodness, wouldn't that create a fuss to the people in this world who tell us we love our dogs too much, humanize their behavior to a sinful level, and really ought to see a shrink? Dog people like us will always meet naysayers like that along the way. But we don't have to agree with them. Although dogs can't think like humans, they certainly can think on some level, and they make choices for their behavior all the time. And some dogs are more "thoughtful" than others, just like we see in the human species.

I'll leave it to others to relate Commander's intelligence and thinking process in the woods. I'll tell you my experience with him in everyday life. On the most basic level, when we let Commander out in the yard to do his business, he was careful to pick a spot on the yard's edge or under a shrub. No embarrassing missteps for this canine or goo-on-the-shoe for his owners. And he never got lost, even when we did. Several times, we got accidently separated from each other, and he was always back at the truck or the camp when we arrived there. The look in his eye always seemed to say, "Don't be so stupid next time. I've been waiting here forever." One time in his later years, when his hearing was not so good, he and I went for a walk on a series of logging roads in Maine. I turned suddenly to see where a skid road went, and he had already gone straight. As I returned to the logging road, I saw him coming back, and I called, whistled, and waved my arms, but he went by like a freight train, retracing our main trail with his nose to the ground. I followed him as fast as I could, calling and whistling, all the way out to the hardtop road. There, I asked some fellows in their dooryard if they saw a white dog. They said a beautiful white dog had been sitting at the entrance to our driveway for a long time as if waiting for someone, ignored their attention, and finally turned and went home. Sure enough, there he was in the dooryard when I got back.

I loved the way Commander didn't waste his time and effort. Our other dogs leap from the tailgate like the charge of the light brigade. Then they run around like they've lost their minds, finally settling down to the task at hand. Commander was never like that. He'd look around, wait until the crazy dogs cleared the area, check to see what we were doing, and then calmly hop down to do his walk, hunt, or whatever. And the only time he retrieved a stick or ball was when the other dogs gave up on its whereabouts. Then he'd casually smell his way to the object and bring it back. He didn't care about the object, but he must have thought that the humans did, or they wouldn't be making such a fuss over getting it back.

Near the end of his life, he tended to tire more easily, and when, at what he considered the end of his day, he'd get on the bed and start a very memorable and endearing series of 3 barks. He'd wait a moment and do it again. Eventually, we'd give up and come to bed, too. He'd thought that through on his own: If I go to bed, they will follow, or I'll make them. And he had also figured out that possession is nine-tenths of the law. If he got on the bed first, all other dogs would have to sleep on the floor.

When he got old and physically feeble, he figured out how to maintain pack leadership. If push came to shove, he could sound fierce. Sharp little teeth were strategically placed if needed. He was careful to watch his backside and not get caught outside his sphere of influence. Push hardly ever came to shove.

Can dogs think? I believe, as do most people who have dogs that they do. I believe it allows us to relate to each other and delight in each other's company.

POINT, FLUSH, WHAT'S FOR LUNCH

During the autumn of Commander's eleventh year, Den returned from a neighborhood hunt with tears in his eyes. That was the day Commander transitioned from a formal "let's go get 'em, lots of 'em, wherever they are and whatever it takes" Setter to a "let's do it after our lunch break" Setter. Although his spirit was willing, he just did not have the strength and stamina of his youth anymore. During this hunt, he had collapsed from weakened hindquarters, that unknown to us since the previous season, had crept in, riding the insidious Father Time. Commander had crawled his way to Dennis with the woodcock that Commander had just pointed, and Dennis had shot. Dennis's tears were from his worry for Commander, but from sadness, also. Time was catching up with his dear, dear friend. An era of excitement and perfection that they had shared these many years was in the early stages of drawing to a close. Although with careful planning and consideration, Commander would hunt for several more years, the best was behind them. I felt so bad for them both.

And yet, my special time with Commander seemed to blossom even further from that point forward. He seemed to sense it was time to retire and look for birds just for fun. It was as if the pressure was gone, like when we humans retire and don't have to get up any certain time, or work any certain hours, or answer the phone anymore. He couldn't hear the phone (whistle) very well anyway.

And so, we started our own era, our era of "walkies." Lots and lots of walkies. Lots of miles together. The more we walked, the more he transitioned from a dog who had to find birds, no matter how far away they were, to a dog that enjoyed smelling his way along a forest road, staying pretty close to me, or checking back in case I was not keeping up. I didn't have to worry about him disappearing into the woods as I once had. He was content to keep me company. As his sight and hearing faded further, we perfected a series of hand signals and kept walking.

If there were any grouse or woodcock along our routes, he'd still find them. His nose never faded like his eyes and ears. But after he went on point, I'd flush the bird, or he would, for the fun of it, and we'd continue on our walk. We always lingered by the old apple trees on the camp road or at the Moosehorn until the ubiquitous grouse were found and flushed. Once, he found a whole flight of woodcock in the alder swamp along our camp road and had a riot pointing and flushing them all in sequence. I just stood still and enjoyed the show from the road. When he had put them all in the air to his satisfaction, he returned to the road so we could continue our walk. Birddog fanciers might find this curious, wondering why he was breaking point and flushing birds. When you have a dog of such talent and expansive experience who has hunted hundreds of days and pointed probably thousands of birds, there comes a time when you realize he'd forgotten more about his business than you'll ever know. Here was a dog who had seen and done it all and was making his own decisions. He knew Den was not coming with the gun, and he had his fun with me watching and smiling. They were sublime moments, realizing I was witnessing the epitome of greatness—he was just having fun with nothing more to prove.

In general, he did not care about following the birds. He pointed and flushed because he had figured out that I was carrying lunch, not a gun. The memorable exception to this rule was a hilarious time on a woods road near our West Virginia home. It was on Jake Hill, to be exact. Catching up to Commander near a big tree on the bank of a wash, I noticed he was on point. As I approached, a big turkey flew up out of the bottom of the wash, scattering the fall leaves, startling us both. The turkey landed and started running through the woods on the adjacent hillside. Commander thought this was too good to be true and started trotting after him, on his stiff old legs. And they just kept going like this, with me jogging along behind, laughing the whole way. The turkey finally got a clue and took flight, leaving us to sit quietly and watch him disappear. There was almost an audible sigh from Commander. We shortly resumed our hike and had our picnic lunch on our favorite log at the hill's crest.

Commander's golden years were a pleasant time for us both. Two retirees, off on jaunts, whenever the mood struck, and the weather cooperated. If we had to run errands instead, he'd ride all day in the back seat. He was a great ride-along buddy. It didn't matter to him if we didn't get to walk. There was always a picnic lunch anyway, with a more than average chance of a cheeseburger showing up.

COFFEE AND DONUTS

A sip of coffee, a bite of donut, I'm browsing through things on my computer as the day starts. I'll always love those donuts. They are a brand we bought at the little store during summers when we're at the lake cottage or "camp," as they are called in Maine. They are always fresh and tasty, each wrapped in its own cellophane pouch, and they have a nice way of going down with a cup of freshly brewed coffee. But that's not what makes them truly unique to me.

When Commander was older, most mornings, he and I would head out for a walk. I took him for a walk almost every day of his old age—even the day he died. We so enjoyed our time poking along and exploring together. As he grew less able to see and hear very well, he stayed close to me for his sense of security. His nose still owned him, but he had changed the way he navigated. The hand signals we had long worked out continued to serve us, but if we became separated for a time, he always knew he could find me by retracing his steps and using his nose.

We loved to walk the gravel woods road about half-mile through the Maine woods to a cove on our lake. As we neared the cove, Commander would come in close to me . . . close enough to hear the crinkle of the cellophane in the pocket of my hooded sweatshirt. He'd wade in the lake and get a drink, then look to me—not for a hand signal, but a piece of donut. Oh dear, on those days when I neglected to bring one, those big brown eyes bored a hole right into my soul. But most mornings, I did have one in my pocket, and we'd sit on the old dock and share our treat. Then we'd sit a while longer, taking in the sights, sounds, and smells of the lake. When my travel mug was emptied of coffee, we'd head home reluctantly, knowing that this wasn't just "coffee and donuts." It was a feast at life's splendid table.

It's been a while now since we lost our Commander, and there have been donuts on the counter now and then every summer. There were five boxes one week, through some human miscommunication and weak moments in the check-out lines. That would be one box for every dog we have now (hasn't our family grown!?) Each of these canine friends enjoys walking down the old woods road with me. We always have a wonderful time, and I enjoy each dog's unique personality and amusing habits. But the walks are just not the same. There's more running around willy-nilly, more growling and competing. I have to pay attention to their whereabouts to keep them out of trouble. No one checks in with me unless I insist on it. And they'd all rather have their donut before we even leave the driveway. No, I don't believe a single donut has made it down to the little dock on the cove.

OLD AGE AND BEAUTY

Commander was always a pleasure to touch. He had beautiful, soft white fur, which did not show any graying as he aged, just a gradual loss of his orange belton freckles. Conversely, the gray hair in my formerly brownish mane stands out like neon:

"Old Age is Coming." As Commander grew older, his hearing got progressively worse, his eyes grew a little cloudy, and he became a little frail and tentative with his step. He wandered a little less far and depended on us a little more. He was much like us humans in our old age, except he was always beautiful, inside and out. Often, I would be on a walk with him, and even when he was 14 and 15, people would see us and remark, "What a beautiful dog!" Wouldn't you like such a compliment when you are that age (i.e., 80 to 90 years in human years)? Dream on! Yes, some people age beautifully and gracefully, but I am not one of them, in the beauty department anyway. I still hold out hope for the graceful part.

I never worried about him getting lost, even with his waning hearing and sight, because his nose was still amazing, and he had used his reasoning skills to figure out that sticking close to us was the right thing to do. There's a special story about this time of Commander's life that Den tells best.

ONE LAST GROUSE

February 28, 2007, was the last day of our West Virginia grouse season, and as was not unusual for that time of year, typically sunny, looking of winter but smelling of spring. Father Time has made a distinct mark on our old friend, and not knowing what another year would bring, we set out with some hope and resolve for "the fields near home."

It's an un-named covert off an un-named road far below the summit of Reddish Knob. There's a gate on this small woods road now, but on this day, we parked at the beginning of the skid trail that leads back and along the South facing ridge. Falling away to the right are several draws that lead to the foot of the ridge, several hundred feet below, scattered patches of shady snow in little islands, the draws holding tight nearly all their snow under pine and laurel. I'd hunted this covert before this winter, and today, with my two-hunt limit per covert, would be the final time, even were the season not ending. Drifter had encountered a group of four grouse, and despite his being in my regular rotation of the dogs, seven years old, and having had hundreds of grouse contacts with me, he'd not been able to pin them in any way that allowed shooting. I will not shoot bumped birds, and we had no luck following them up. Looking back, that seems a bit providential.

With a decent breeze working its way up the ridge, Commander did not feel the need to drop into every draw as we worked out its spine. Typical of him, he could hunt acres with his astonishing nose, heading off only when the faint aroma of quarry told him. As we made further down the road, where a draw opened at the top of the ridge, he made an easy right turn, dropping down the draw on the near side. Watching him disappear into the thickening laurel, I followed him, and as the draw narrowed a bit, he slanted left toward the deepest part, his bell stopping, the beeper coming on. Knowing this old boy made no mistakes, I came in behind him and readied the gun. One more step and suddenly there were birds in the air, though I could only see one. Firing once, then anxiously again, it seemed there was a flinch, and the bird was circling back to my left, curiously but seemingly unharmed.

Commander and I moved off straight ahead, but he turned and worked back left as if he was just as curious as I. After a couple of dozen yards, he locked up, and I moved past him, expecting the bird, likely wounded as it now occurred to me, to fly or be fleeing on foot. But as I got six or eight paces past Commander, I realized he'd not moved, a familiar indication that I need to go back. Peering down at the base of some tangled laurel stems, there was the mortally wounded, but very much alive, grouse. Commander knew the difference between hot scent and a dead bird and had dutifully pointed. But when I said simply "dead," he plunged his head down and came up with the bird. It was a euphoric moment, more than ever, as I look back on it. He'd embodied everything he had been to us over all the years, one last time putting all his talent and prowess to its highest and best use, making it look easy, and especially so as he moved with a simple, modest gait in cover, hunting within himself, making cover through which he once bounded, brains, instinct, and experience coming together for that beautiful moment. Stac had come in behind all this. I continued walking back past Commander after I called dead, to a slightly open sunny spot in the laurel and now turned to kneel for the retrieve, Stac's camera catching multiple frames.

We had done it all right off the bat. But Commander was not done, and he moved off directly, heading out across the other side of the draw. While I was gushing to Stac and reliving the moment in my mind, I didn't realize that Commander had just locked up under the laurel yet again, and my one more step put up another grouse that was an easy shot if I'd been paying attention. But that was O.K. We'd killed one of the three, perhaps four, and that would be enough. Still, Commander was not done, and he continued to course the draw, the coming ridge and showing no signs of quitting.

By this time, the dog mommy felt like we needed to call him in, as she was very sensitive about his "overdoing it." So, we repaired to the road along the ridge, now only hearing Commander's bell, and realized he could not hear our voices or the whistle. I held up my hand and said to Stac that we should just stop here and wait. Sure enough, slowly but surely, we could tell the bell was moving back around us to one side. We continued to wait, the southerly breeze on our right cheek. The bell came in and out of hearing, still making back on us. Gradually, the wind carried the bell off our right shoulder, then to our rear, and then off our left shoulder, it came quickly, directly, from downwind behind us. In moments our dear old friend was back. While we fretted, he'd decided to hunt a bit more and, using his powerful nose, simply worked around on the breeze until he found our scent line and followed it in.

We gloried in that day, resting under a tall white pine, taking more photos, our dear boy having a drink of chunks of slowly melting, granular snow his mommy gave him in handfuls. Thankful for the beauty of it all, our little family of three, together in those endless mountains we once called home.

———

And so it was. When all the summer residents were gone, Commander and I would prowl the neighborhood at dusk. We loved to walk at night through the quiet camp settlement, along the dark little roads between the empty buildings. One minute he'd be next to me; the next minute, he'd disappear. Straining my eyes, I'd see him as a flash of white beside this camp and that, poking his nose where it didn't belong, marking this corner and that shrub. He knew where I was, but I had to work hard to keep track of him. When I'd had enough of his shenanigans, I stood still until I caught a glimpse of him (usually far away), and I would run after him and gently grab him, which startled him back to the reality of returning home for the night. But he'd kept track of me all the while, that beautiful nose that never quit.

But in general, his circle of comfort shrank in size, and he drew closer to Dennis and me physically and emotionally. He wanted to sleep right between us on the bed as a safeguard against marauding canine intruders or inadvertently falling off the bed in the throes of really deep old dog sleep. This had happened a few times, and it wasn't funny when it did, especially to Commander. He was known to slide down between a bed and the wall once in a while and get stuck on his back like a turtle until we could rescue him. If that happened to one of us, we would be pretty freaked out, wouldn't we? Or hurt. But not him. He'd wait there calmly, legs up until we frantically bumbled around to move the bed and get him out. He'd been so far into dreamland that he was just waking up. We often wished we could sleep so deeply.

So, there he stayed between us on our little full-sized mattress. It was a peaceful nocturnal existence if one did not mind the draft of a short-sheeted backside. Or the dog dreams. And I am not talking about those cute little dreams in which dogs flail their legs for a minute and whine a few times. Commander's dreams must have been magnificent!! He wasn't just twitching for a few moments; he was running full bore. He often ran a marathon on Den's back for several minutes, sometimes driving poor husband to the couch. It was pretty funny, but it did not allow us to sleep very well. So, we tried some creative solutions to keep Commander close and safe during the night while giving us more peace and quiet. We purchased a nice cot from Cabela's, the same height as the bed, and coaxed him onto it. He didn't care for it. Next, we built a 3x3 sleeping platform next to the bed and put a nice dog mattress on it. He'd humor us by staying there until we were asleep, then he'd tiptoe over in between us and call it a night. Eventually, since we couldn't bear the only other option of tying him up somewhere, we just gave in.

The shrinking of physical distance corresponds with the world of emotions in both humans and canines. In Commander's case, his love and devotion to us became pure white, like his fur. Maybe when Dennis and I hit our Golden Years, one of us will be sent to the cot or adjacent sleeping quarters for snoring, snorting, or running in our sleep. I can understand now why old people often get twin beds or twin rooms! But then again, maybe knowing that your time together on this earth is finite and speeding away makes you want to overlook the little irritations and disruptions and snuggle up close. My parents have been married a hundred thousand years (well, 70 to be exact), and they still snuggle up at night.

Being so close to us in his old age meant it was hard on him when we left him for very long, and when we were home, he depended on us completely and without question. Den used to tell me, "he'd walk by me three times trying to find you in the house." We had a special thing, for sure. He depended on us for his comfort and safety, even when underwater!! The turtle-on-its-back episode reminds me that one time when he was wide awake, he got himself into a legs-up situation from a fall. We were all, people and dogs, on the waterfront, and he was following us out the ramp to the floating dock when he got bumped off the dock into the lake by one of the other dogs. There he was, upside down in the shallow water, looking up at us with an astonished expression. And even then, he didn't panic but waited for us to wade in and help him get vertical so he could walk to the shore, looking completely embarrassed. Again, not too funny to him, but we still chuckled.

Because he trusted us to do the right thing for him, he put up with many visits to veterinarians, tests of all kinds, and a constant barrage of pills, remedies, and special diets. In exchange, we knew his love for us was unfaltering. He was always there for company, and he was constantly entertaining us with his canine wit and intelligence. You don't think dogs have some kind of special sensory system above the human scale? I do. Often, when I was worried or shedding a tear over something, he would find me, figure out that something was wrong and apply his furry medical treatment.

Do you remember how we have been joking throughout this account of our life with Commander that Dennis may have been using him as a Chick Magnet way back when? I hate to disappoint, but even Dennis will admit that Commander was a beautiful dog, a beautiful friend, right up to his last day on earth. Girls stopping to admire his dog—were doing just that.

CHEETOS AND CHERRY COKE:
THE END OF OUR TIME TOGETHER

I refuse to detail the medical twists and turns of Commander's fall from the physical world into the netherworld of tears and memories. I hate books that make you want to cry or throw up because the great dog, the hero of the story, and the whole reason the book was written dies a horrible death or has to be "put to sleep." The way Commander died was this: Between the ages of 14 and 15, he had several problems as his body started to grow too old for this world, and in the end, one must say it was simply old age. The particulars don't matter very much at this point. What matters is that we did the very best we could for him without crossing the line into undue pain and suffering for him, and he was an amazingly strong-willed dog. He left us at nearly 15 ½ but only when he knew he just couldn't "win" this one last battle. He died in my arms, and I was grateful I was there with him as he took his last breath.

A year earlier, he survived a long and complicated surgery to remove a 6.5-pound splenetic mass. We applaud the surgeon, Dr. Julie Keene, at Veazie Veterinary Clinic in Maine. She is brilliant, and we are grateful to her and all the people who monitored and orchestrated Commander's recovery, 24 hours a day for the week after surgery. He had quite a struggle for a while, as his body tried to reset itself, and I stayed with him every hour that I could, laying in his big hospital "suite" reading a book, watching him, trying to get him to eat and drink a little. But it was finally Dennis' arrival from a fishing trip cut short that caused something to click in his head, infused him with enough gumption to nip at the technician, and head for the ride home to the lake and his normal life. Despite several nay-sayers and statistics to the contrary, he lived another thirteen wonderful months, finally giving it up to complications from gastric torsion emergency surgery. Even if he had survived the bumbling of this veterinarian, I feel that other things were happening in his old body that were signaling the end.

Recently, I was wasting time while waiting to pick up Max, Commander's son, from surgery to remove an icky tumor from under his tail. His surgeon had warned me that the look, feel, and position of it probably meant . . . and here's that horrible, heart-wrenching, gut-liquifying word . . . malignant. As I pretended to look through the museum where I was wasting time, I thought about that 6.5-pound tumor of Commander's and how people always asked if it was malignant. Guess what, way back then, when asked if we wanted to have it analyzed at the lab, we said "no." It only took a brief conversation between Dennis and myself to come to a mutual conclusion that we did not want to know. We figured that if it were (the m-word), the disease would progress and kill

Commander, but we could live happily until the end of his time. If it weren't, well, then we would all just live happily.

That m-word is the most horrible word in our language. I wonder if there is an equally strong but opposite word in our language that means "spreads and permeates through an organism in a fantastically good way?" A good kind of metastasis? As humans, we might live to the end of our lives in a better way when we know that time is limited. But as caregivers to our pets, maybe we can put a better face forward not knowing. Dogs are quite well versed in reading and responding to our moods and emotions, a sixth sense of sorts. I don't know about you, but I am really bad at faking my emotions. So, life went on for many happy months—well over a year, until old age simply caught up with Commander. We walked at least twice a day, and took countless road trips, and did a lot of cheeseburgers in the drive-up window together. It felt like it would go on forever, but of course, it couldn't. God doesn't allow anything to go on forever because that would cut short the following generations of really great experiences. The new great things in our lives certainly can't replace the old, but they are themselves great in their own space and time. And, in turn, we grow and learn to love in new and different ways.

When times are tough for me, I turn to my favorite comfort foods . . . Cheetos and Cherry Coke. When I don't feel like eating anything else, I can usually nibble on these. And just buying them always brings the slightest smile to my face, like sharing an inside joke with myself. On Commander's last day on this earth, I went to see him in the recovery area at the veterinarian's place. I just sat with him a long time, touched him, talked with him, and generally just let him know I was there and that he was loved, loved, loved. After a few hours, I knew in my heart of hearts that he would not recover from this latest affront to his physical self, and I decided to take a break for an hour to feed my soul and think about his life and friendship. I found myself sitting at the end of a very long dock, looking out at the saltwater, and having a little Cherry Coke and a few Cheetos. A little while later, as the afternoon started to fade, I unwrapped myself from my thoughts, stood up on stiffened limbs, and returned to Commander. I curled up next to him, told him it was OK to go, and thanks for all the greatness he brought to our lives. Within minutes, his breath just sort of evened out and then stopped altogether. He was the perfect dog right up to the last minute. I cried, mostly for myself, and I am crying now as I write this, even though it was years ago.

Y'know, the funny thing about Cherry Coke and Cheetos? Commander would share burgers, fries, chicken nuggets, cheese, and a million other things with me, but he never cared for a Cheeto. I would throw one back to him where he loved to ride, on the back seat of the truck, and I would always find it later, all mashed up and uneaten. My two new ride-along-dogs, Nifty the Border Collie and Max, Commander's son, love Cheetos! That's by design, I guess: a new generation of life companions and loves. And speaking of Max—that tumor on his tail? Benign! Live on.

KICK IN THE STOMACH FROM THE ONCE-IN-A-LIFETIME DOG

Given our lifestyle and the number of dogs we've incorporated into our home, we have come to know lots of veterinarians. One of our favorite and most trusted veterinarians was Dr. Julie Keene, whom we met through Commander. She is the kind of vet who listens to what you have to say and sits down right on the floor to hear what your pet has to say. Then, whether she agrees with your unprofessional ramblings or not, she takes matters into her own very professional hands and does the very best job she can. Who could ask for more? More than once, she helped us bring Commander back from "a bad place" and gave us the gift of more time with him.

After he died, she took the time to write a personal letter and picked out a special card to send us. I visited her one day with another of our dogs, and I was still really struggling with my grief for Commander. She told me that Commander was probably our once in a lifetime dog and that given enough time, we'd wake up and not feel the kick in the stomach quite so much. Gradually, that sick feeling would be replaced by wonderful memories flowing in like a warm ocean tide. She lost four dear pets that same year. And, although she had helped plenty of people through their final time with their beloved pets, she said it was different when the pets were her own, and she was surprised at how difficult it was.

That phrase "lifetime dog" was new to me, but I now realize that anyone who has owned dogs will be able to conjure up memories of that one dog that rose above the rest. There is an unusually close connection or bond with that dog and mutual love, admiration, and respect that . . . well, quite frankly, is hard to explain. It's sort of like the purest form of love. The lifetime dog would be especially hard to explain to someone who is not a "dog person." The only thing I can wish for them is that someday, somewhere, somehow, they are lucky enough to have a lifetime dog of their own.

A dog's life is not very long in comparison to the average human life. So, consider this: your chance of getting a remarkable dog may be proportional to how many dogs you take care of in your life and how well you get to know them. Whether or not you succeed in finding a lifetime dog may also be a factor of where you are in your life, the time you have to spend with your dog, and how much you need a companion. Really? No, that's a bunch of hooey.

Those factors only play a role in whether you realize what you have on the end of the leash or tied to the doghouse outside. The thing about dogs is this: you need to leave yourself open to them, to let them be a part of your everyday human life. Only then can you receive the gift of the lifetime dog when it comes your way. There is no other reason for the species dog to walk this earth except to be with man. And yes, some of us love them in a big way . . . and that's OK. Dennis and I believe that's what the creator had in mind.

In this house, at this moment in time, we have five canine friends. If we were so lucky to have all of them until age 15, we'd be 70-something. But, let's face it, we'll always be putting another in the rotation, so we'll be more like 90-something with one or both feet in the grave before we run out of dogs. But so far, apologies all around; none have been quite as amazing as Commander. Commander's constant presence centered and guided Dennis for fifteen plus years in ways that only the two of them can know. I only shared Commander's life for eight years, but they were wonderful years, and we made up for the lost time. He was a godsend to us both.

Sometimes I think about the next years and the anticipated heartache . . . dogs leaving us, elderly parents leaving us, our loved ones with poor health . . . I can get really low thinking about all that at once. Sometimes I lay in bed at night thinking about how fast the day just went by, frustrated that I wasted it doing nothing good, or worse, deliberately made it bad by losing my temper or thinking negatively about something. To save me from myself those nights, I play a little mind game. First, I list everything I did poorly that day, everything I could certainly improve upon, and how I could have handled the situation or event more positively. Next, I think about all the good things that happened that day, including those that made someone else's life better, furry or human. And so it goes for grief, whether it's for a human or a pet. We keep our column of happy things next to the sadness column, adding to the happy column until it overpowers the sadness. Maybe that's why it is important for Dennis and me to write this account of our lifetime dog so that we can replace his absence with the immortal gift that was his life. And if someone else reads this, they will, in turn, remember their canine blessings and enjoy our tale, too.

When we were young.

Living and Loving: The good life on the couch was Puppy's. Well-earned, well-deserved, he knew on what side his bread was buttered.

A tenth birthday celebration, "Meat Cake." You can tell the old boy is saying "give it to me!"

In his fourteenth year, perfection had long ago become ordinary. Last grouse—the celebration of a life as it was meant to be lived.

Taking a "snow break."

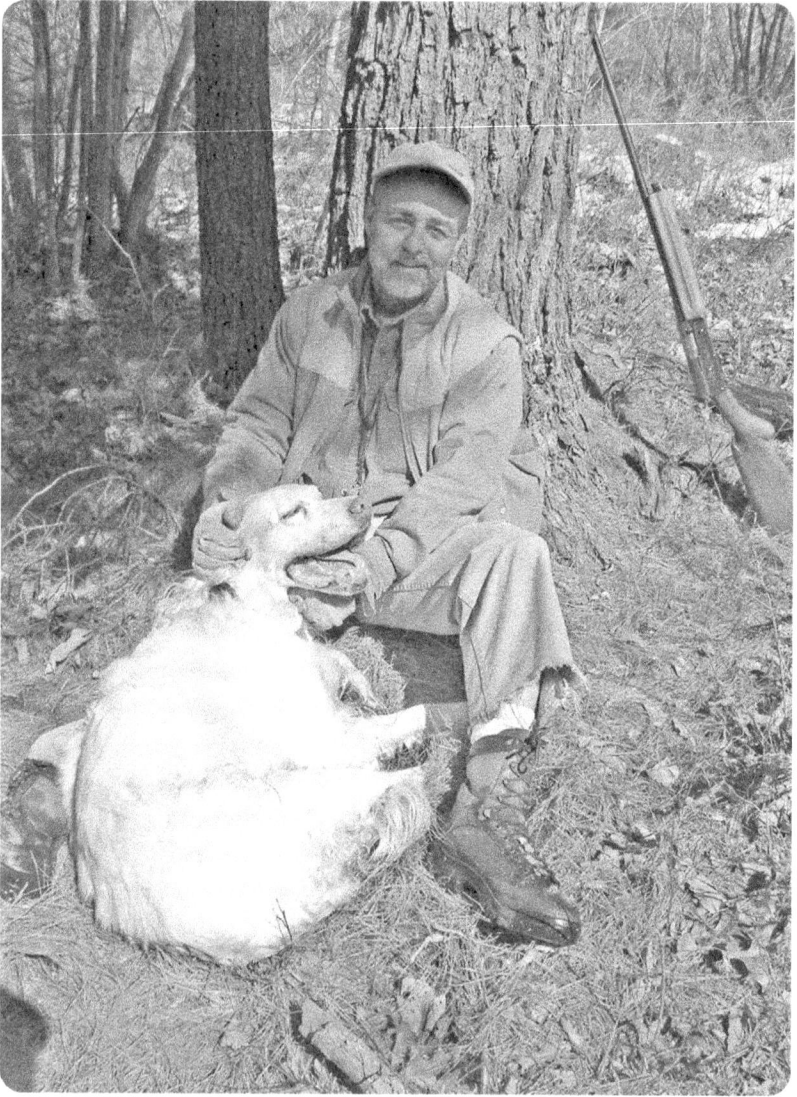

Reveling in the goodness of it all.

AFTERWORD

AS I WRITE this, it's now been more than three years since our dear Commander left us and this life. Despite that passage of time, the power of my emotions—happy and sad—can overpower me when I see something that was his, think of some special moment, and perhaps most profound of all, realize that our time together, something that seemed unending then—is gone. We have some wonderful, talented, beautiful dogs that bring much joy to our lives. Our oldest, Shadbush Rymans Maxwel, Commander's son, never worked out as a hunter. We gave him away to friends when it became clear that his highly dominant father would not tolerate him for reasons we never knew. He's the senior dog now. There is Crooked Stump Drifter, a large, orange belton who, though never a superstar, was and remains a very good, solid bird dog and as he approached his dotage, seems to be ever closer to us. Ruffwood Chance, a very talented grouse dog that even Bill has suggested might, might be comparable to Puppy. He's wowed many a hunting companion, but in our hearts, we still know Puppy was the best. Finally, there is Ruffwood Captain Magic, from a single puppy litter thrown by our Drifter, who, with one line back to Corey Ford's October, Corey's last dog, is a stunning example in every way of what a first-class companion Setter is supposed to be. We are blessed with extraordinary dogs, dear friends, companions, and hunters. But the experience of Commander, all that he was, and in our hearts, continues to eclipse all else. Stacy coming into our lives when she did was a godsend for both of us, and especially so for Commander, for the beauty of the bonding, the loving ritual of their lives, was for me, something unmatched to witness.

In 2009, approaching our tenth year of retirement, we decided to make good on a process of deliberation we promised ourselves as we approached a decade of our Maine/West Virginia retirement lifestyle. After duly considering many factors across the board, we determined to re-locate to the northwestern U.S, specifically, central Oregon. While the anticipation of something new, different, and exciting captured our imagination and took us west, I am not without my wistful moments, being an easterner by birth and for the then fifty-seven years of my life. In my quiet moments, then, anyone would understand that leaving was so much more than "just leaving."

Above the mantlepiece of the gas fireplace in the master bedroom suite of our new home in Oregon is a plain wooden sign, sage green with black lettering reading simply "Home Is Where Your Dog Is." Below that sign on the mantlepiece is a mauve colored satin bag containing a simple earthen urn in which rests one-half of the cremains of our beloved Commander. The other half is interred below a rock under a large Hemlock where I photographed, he and my friend Bill with Commander's first point-flush-kill deep in the Virginia hills, and where Bill and I went, alone, to bury him. The fusion of those experiences brought me back to that place just a few weeks before we headed west. That chilly late November day, Bill and I committed his spirit to the woods that were his realm, reading over him:

> In the presence of Dennis J. LaBare and William P. "Bill" Horn on 20 November 2008 in Vance's Cove, Frederick County, Virginia.
>
> Today, we are gathered to remember and give thanks to an Almighty God for Cokesbury's Commander, known affectionately also as Commander Alexander, Puppy, Pie Man, Sweet Pie, and Pie LaBare.
>
> We celebrate Commander's life as a peerless hunter whose talent and passion in the pursuit of grouse

so thrilled and amazed us. We are here to return ½ of his earthly remains to the ground upon which a special moment in his and our lives occurred and was recorded thirteen years and three days ago and is remembered by us here today. We ask a merciful God to grant our request to return to these wild mountains his hunting spirit, to keep and protect it here, along with the grouse, the wildest of wild things, he once pursued here.

While we marveled at Commander for all the wonderful things he did, we remember him most of all for his being our friend. He will live in our hearts forever, always with the hope of sharing his sweet companionship again one day.

Until then,

Rest in Peace

———

I don't know if I'm capable of summing up the full meaning and impact Commander had on my life. The direction that the world took for me was a trajectory completely different than anything that could have resulted without him. The first and most important was Stacy and I beginning to make a life together several years after she and I first met, but a meeting that was possible only because of Puppy. While it's all taken together in memory, I have to stop and sort out what Commander helped me see and feel just between him and me. In the time of the hunt, it was that a man and a dog could share the wonder of the woods, the hills, and the interaction of our souls, a seeking and finding of a beauty that never would have been possible without us together. There was a bond to form between Stacy and Puppy, one with beauty, depth, and tenderness that struck me as one that only a dog and a woman could share, and it was just what was the very best for Puppy's future—and mine. As time passed, Stacy and I built the life that was completely additive to each of us, especially with Puppy, as we shared what seemed like Time unlimited. Truly, for us, "Home is where our dog is." More than anything else, though, in mine and Puppy's time together, he caused my heart to open to the warmth and beauty that can exist between a man and a dog. What started as a desire to have a nice hunting dog became "the rest of my life," and I would not trade anything for that. On many quiet days here in the room where our dazzling western view of the mighty Cascades is best, I often wander around to gaze at the little framed pictures of special moments with all of our dogs, mostly photos of their first grouse or woodcock over a point. But with Puppy, there are moments captured that are just moments, when somewhere within, Stac and I knew we needed to record a day, a grouse or 'cock taken, the slanting afternoon light of mid-February—whatever struck us—so special in those mountains we then called home. Of all the little photo keepsakes we have, it is those of Puppy where I linger the longest, gazing into his eyes, reliving the moment as I'm able to recall it from so many, many years and days afield. I don't know where I'd be without him in this life, and frankly, I don't care to know. I've lived it all, as George Bird Evans said it in his book title with "A Dog, A Gun, and Time Enough." It's just that there is no such thing as "Time Enough."

My life during my working years when it was just Puppy and me, in the basement office with some smooth jazz playing, Puppy near my feet—while I'm in such a good place right now—those were very good days. I was in no hurry to leave, though that leaving brought Stacy and for Puppy and me, a whole new world of love and contentment for us both. I had my home, my business, Puppy, enough money to take care of myself and build a future—there was no downside, but Puppy and I landed in tall cotton, even beyond the bliss we knew before she came. I know now that wanting to be back there again for the very largest part is not truly regressive, but wistful, fitful, happy remembrance of very good days. The lyrics of a popular song come to mind when the grief I still feel for his not being here now fills my heart . . .

"Last thing I remember, I was running for the door. I had to find the passage back to the place I was before . . ."

He came to me in the flower of my middle age, changed everything in my life for the better, and when he left, I had become an old man, so I had to go there, to his quiet place in the woods where he worked his magic on me, Stacy, Bill, and the birds . . .

ONE LAST TIME

(This essay appeared previously in *The Pointing Dog Journal*)

His PLACE IS a bit of a drive from here. Not a big drive, something over an hour, a little over sixty miles. But I need to see him, as soon, it will be nearly three thousand miles, and with special friends, you have to go, to see them once more in person, to look at them and know you've seen all the years, last.

Pulling off the pavement, I start down into the cove, and with the afternoon shadows lengthening, and in the cool of the forest, I open the truck windows and drive un-hurriedly. It's a pretty woods, the road descending gradually, the slope on my right seeming to make North Mountain rise as I follow the gently winding road down, down, the oaks, hickories, and pines gradually enveloping my descent. Tiny at first, a stream is gathering its headwaters on my left, and in slowing on some turns, I can hear the squeak of August crickets. The drought is showing its hand, no laughing riffles, but languid pools, motionless runs.

The two- and three-quarter miles in, and I have to stop and walk. His is a private place, and the gate is closed. It's quiet here now. The walk is crickets chirping, an occasional locust or katydid rattling somewhere high overhead, a small plane drones faintly— the sound of woods in late summer. Near a solitary apple tree, and though a little fruit is hanging, there is nothing on the ground. But at my approach, no deer scampers, no grouse flushes, just the rhythmic sound of my shoes on crushed stone.

I've passed the little power line. I know I'm getting close, the Multiflora, Autumn Olive, and small hardwoods pressing in on the road. There, suddenly, is his trail, barely a trace, trying desperately to grow over, and I'm looking for the tree by his place. We did a picture on his first bird, and under that tree, one could easily see far into Old Virginia, your gaze guarded by the brow of Paddy Mountain, into the distant Shenandoah. The last time I visited him was in the late fall, and the open woods made it easy to spot the crown of the big hemlock that marked his place, but now, as I penetrate the darkening woods, I can't see it, and I am panicked. I walk, turn, take a few hasty steps. It must be here. It's not that far from the gravel road. I walk back out and retrace my steps. There it is. So different now. Year by year, spring by summer, the forest is closing in inexorably, and there is no view to the distant valley. But he is there.

Kneeling, I put my hands on his stone and remember the day we brought him here for the last time. Memories and tears. How did it all get by so fast? In my grief, I call out to him . . . I must turn him . . . the last cast was wide, "ho, Puppy, ho!" I call, but the forest is quiet, the crickets silent, the shadows descending. I'm sure I hear the leaves rustling in his gait. Standing, I call again I'm sure I've seen him turn, his snowy white flank gleaming in the last rays of the afternoon sun. Now he's by my side once more. Late at night, as he slept between us, I would run my hand over his occipital, impressing the feel of it into the lifeline of my hand, and I can feel that impression now, his nearness again. The light is fading, and it's time to get back. But the cover near the power line is good. I turn to bring him along, but he is gone. He's taking just one more turn. I want to go to him, last.

To the memory of
Cokesbury's Commander
22 May 1993 – 11 August 2008
There could never be another!

ABOUT THE AUTHORS

DENNIS JAMES LABARE was born July 30, 1953, in Baltimore, Maryland. His father casually raised him as a hunter but as a serious fly fisherman. His education, graduating from the University of Maine in 1977 and Towson State University in 1986 with a B.S. and an M.S. in Biology/Stream Ecology, was driven largely by those interests. LaBare operated his environmental consulting firm and, along the way, managed to put in forty-one years of dedicated voluntaryism to Trout Unlimited and the Ruffed Grouse Society. In 1993, he was awarded National Trout Unlimited's then-highest award for a volunteer, Trout Conservation Award—Non-Professional. He is the author of *Tagewahnahn—The Landlocked Salmon at Grand Lake Stream* (2007) and was Special Project Director for *A Passion for Grouse* (Wild River Press, 2013). His other publication credits include *The Pointing Dog Journal, The Retriever Journal, Pennsylvania Angler and Boater, The Angler's Journal, Virtual Fly Shop*, and a chapter in *The Guide to Trout Fishing in Maryland and South-Central Pennsylvania*. His photography has appeared in *The Virginia Sportsman*. His greatest achievement was marrying Helen Stacy Miller in 2001.

WILLIAM P. "BILL" HORN, ESQ, was born in Delaware on December 16, 1950, and completed his undergraduate and legal education at The American University in 1972 and 1983. He was a Congressional Staffer for the old House Interior Committee (now the Natural Resources Committee) in the 1970s. During the Reagan Administration, he was Deputy Under Secretary of the Interior and subsequently Assistant Secretary for Fish, Wildlife, and Parks. At the end of the Administration in 1989, Horn entered private practice, becoming a nationally respected attorney in wildlife, endangered species, public land law, and sportsman's interests. He helped form the DC chapter of the Ruffed Grouse Society and avidly pursued grouse and woodcock with his late Ryman-type English Setter, Shadbush Feathers. He and LaBare met in 1988, whereupon they became regular gunning partners and friends. Horn is the author of the acclaimed *Seasons on the Flats—An Angler's Year in the Florida Keys* (Stackpole / Headwaters, 2012) and a contributor to *A Passion for Grouse* (Wild River Press, 2013). His periodical work has appeared in *The Pointing Dog Journal*, *American Angler*, and *Florida Sportsman*. He divides his year between Idaho and the Florida Keys with his wife and Ryman-type Setter, Aspen.

HELEN STACY MILLER LABARE was born in Rochester, Minnesota, on October 2, 1955, daughter of the late Ross Hayes Miller, M.D., the internationally renowned neurosurgeon at the Mayo Clinic. She entered only the second class of women at Dartmouth College in 1973 as Valedictorian of her high school class and graduated with honors in 1977. At Dartmouth, her Geography major included classical training in cartography, with which she has contributed to seven books, maps, or cartographic illustration. She attended the University of Maine for an M.S. in Forestry, specializing in mapping and remote sensing. Her career included time in both industrial and consulting forestry, land planning, and environmental review. She retired from MNCPPC-Prince Georges County, Maryland, in 2000. She has hiked, biked, kayaked, and skied all over the world ever since. When she's not, she lives with the LaBare setters and her Border Collie and Australian Shepherd at Setterville near the foot of the Great Smokies in East Tennessee.